MW00776551

Composition and Cognition

The University of California Press gratefully acknowledges publication support from the American Musicological Society.

The publisher and the University of California Press Foundation also gratefully acknowledge the generous support of the Constance and William Withey Endowment Fund in History and Music.

Composition and Cognition

*Reflections on Contemporary Music
and the Musical Mind*

Fred Lerdahl

UNIVERSITY OF CALIFORNIA PRESS

University of California Press, one of the most
distinguished university presses in the United States,
enriches lives around the world by advancing scholarship
in the humanities, social sciences, and natural sciences. Its
activities are supported by the UC Press Foundation and
by philanthropic contributions from individuals and
institutions. For more information, visit www.ucpress.edu.

University of California Press
Oakland, California

© 2020 by Fred Lerdahl

Library of Congress Cataloging-in-Publication Data

Names: Lerdahl, Fred, 1943- author.
Title: Composition and cognition : reflections on
   contemporary music and the musical mind / Fred
   Lehdahl.
Description: Oakland, California : University of
   California Press, [2020] | Includes bibliographical
   references and index. |
Identifiers: LCCN 2019007500 (print) |
   LCCN 2019009894 (ebook) | ISBN 9780520973251
   (ebook) | ISBN 9780520305090 (cloth : alk. paper) |
   ISBN 9780520305106 (pbk. : alk. paper)
Subjects: LCSH: Music—Psychological aspects. |
   Composition (Music) | Musical analysis. | Musical
   perception. | Music theory.
Classification: LCC ML3830 (ebook) | LCC ML3830.L367 2020
   (print) | DDC 781.1—dc23
LC record available at https://lccn.loc.gov/2019007500

Manufactured in the United States of America

29 28 27 26 25 24 23 22 21 20
10 9 8 7 6 5 4 3 2 1

For my wife, Louise Litterick

CONTENTS

For most of my professional life I have worn two hats, one as a composer and the other as a music theorist. My pattern has been to alternate between these two activities, never engaging in both at the same time because they are so different intellectually and emotionally. Yet they are deeply intertwined in my work as a whole. In a few instances, I have touched on their relationship, notably in the articles "Cognitive Constraints on Compositional Systems" (Lerdahl 1988a) and "Composing Notes" (Lerdahl 1999). But for the most part I have kept quiet about the connection. Like many composers, I have a sense of privacy about the creative process. Besides, a piece of music ought to be able to stand on its own without verbal justification. Similarly, it has seemed inappropriate to burden with creative and aesthetic issues the cognitive music theories that I have developed. Social factors also inhibited discussion of the connection between composition and theory. Composer colleagues were dismayed that I spent so much time on theory. Colleagues in the cognitive science of music were puzzled that I abandoned the field for years at a time in order to concentrate on composing. I felt split between the two cultures and found it expedient to avoid one when dealing with the other.

Despite these inhibitions, I have felt all along the need to explain how, for me, composing and theorizing are complementary and indeed mutually necessary activities. My motivation is partly that I wish to be understood in the round. More important, the issues that I have confronted are widely if tacitly experienced by others, and their discussion may be useful.

An invitation to give the Ernest Bloch Lectures in fall 2011 at the University of California at Berkeley offered the opportunity to contemplate publicly the two sides of my career. This book is based on these lectures. I have kept the format and basic content of the talks intact—five chapters for five lectures, none very long. The tone of the book, like that of the lectures, is often informal and personal. Chapter 1 gives an account of my early compositional crisis and subsequent turn to cognitive music theory in order to build a fresh foundation for compositional thinking. Chapter 2 provides an overview of my cognitive theories of tonal music, using a short piece by Schubert as illustration. Chapter 3 takes a selective tour through the nature of the musical mind. Chapter 4 reconsiders "Cognitive Constraints on Compositional Systems" to address anew the gap between compositional method and perceived result that is endemic in contemporary music. Chapter 5 surveys my compositional methods in light of the previous chapters.

I have tried to keep the discussion from becoming too technical and made the accompanying musical figures as uncomplicated as possible. Even so, nonprofessional readers may find parts of the book difficult to follow, in particular chapters 2 and 5. Although the book has an overall arc, each chapter stands to some extent on its own, and for those readers it may be advantageous to focus on the other chapters.

Audio tracks for my compositions that are discussed in the book can be found at the book's University of California Press webpage at www .ucpress.edu/9780520305106. *Music of Fred Lerdahl*, vols. 1–6, can be found at https://www.bridgerecords.com/collections/catalog-all/Fred-Lerdahl. In addition, many of my pieces, as well as works by other composers referred to in the book, are accessible at general internet sites such as iTunes, Spotify, and YouTube.

ACKNOWLEDGMENTS

I am deeply grateful to the Department of Music at the University of California at Berkeley for inviting me to give the Bloch Lectures. The entire faculty supported my semester there, notably Benjamin Brinner, Ed Campion, Richard Taruskin, Bonnie Wade, and above all the late David Wessel. He participated actively in the weekly graduate seminar on composition and cognition that I gave in tandem with the public lectures, and his insights and criticisms helped in writing this book.

I have held three similar graduate seminars at my own institution, Columbia University. Students chose specific topics that they researched under my guidance, leading to class presentations and term papers on many topics within the broad theme of composition and cognition. Their discussions and papers enriched and enlarged my own understanding of the issues.

Joel Gressel, Huck Hodge, Ray Jackendoff, Louise Litterick, Eric Moe, Matthew Ricketts, and David Temperley read the book manuscript and made valuable suggestions that improved its content and style. At the University of California Press, I am grateful to Raina Polivka, Madison Wetzell, Francisco Reinking, and Dawn Hall. David Bird assisted in the final preparation of some of the musical figures.

Occasionally I have borrowed or adapted figures and text from previous publications (Lerdahl 1987, 1988a, 1999, 2001b, 2008, 2009). I gratefully acknowledge permissions from *Contemporary Music Review, Current Musicology, Music Perception,* and Oxford University Press. I also gratefully acknowledge Bridge Records, New World Records, Eighth Blackbird, Naxos Records, and the Saint Paul Chamber Orchestra for permissions to make recordings of my music available through the book's University of California Press website.

Fred Lerdahl

CONVENTIONS AND ABBREVIATIONS USED IN THIS BOOK

CONVENTIONS

Keys (or tonal centers) are indicated in **boldface.**
Major keys are indicated in UPPER CASE.
Minor keys are indicated in lower case.

ABBREVIATIONS

GTTM: *A Generative Theory of Tonal Music*
TPS: *Tonal Pitch Space*
CCCS: "Cognitive Constraints on Compositional Systems"

CHAPTER ONE

From Composition to Theory

I became a music theorist in order to find solutions to compositional issues. After some early success as a composer, at the age of twenty-six I hit a prolonged creative block. My first publishable pieces had been composed in a largely intuitive manner, supplemented by basic motivic and intervallic techniques. Figure 1.1 gives the beginning of *Wake* (1968), for soprano and chamber ensemble. All the pitches in the melody belong to one of the two all-interval tetrachords, marked on the lower staff by brackets. The accented notes at syllable onsets form the identical tetrachord class, shown by the stemmed notes. The intervallic cell is nested within itself. Already I was beginning to think hierarchically. Yet these intervallic relations seemed insufficient and ad hoc. I sought a more comprehensive way to proceed.

Looking to famous composers of the day—that is, of the 1960s— deepened my uncertainty. Elliott Carter was composing very complicated music that made sense in a broad dramatic way but not in its details. Pierre Boulez, after years of presuming to dictate the future of music, was spending most of his time conducting while his own music narrowed in scope and expression. Iannis Xenakis's stochastic methods did not provide enough meaningful distinctions. Luciano Berio's music was talented but weakly structured. Karlheinz Stockhausen had gone

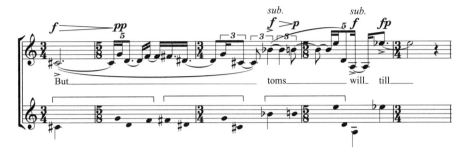

Figure 1.1. Nested motivic treatment at the beginning of *Wake*.

through so many phases that I could no longer take him seriously. The scene was confusing and dispiriting.

Milton Babbitt, the dominant figure at Princeton when I studied there, had provided a close-up model of what it could mean to compose with a system. But his serial system was opaque to perception. Why compose by a hidden code that could be deciphered only with difficulty, and why pretend that musical relations resulting from it were, as he claimed, significant? He tried to support the claim with scientific rhetoric borrowed from logical positivism, a school of philosophy concerned with empirical criteria for the verification of scientific propositions.[1] To say that something is significant, however, is to make a value judgment, and value judgments were of peripheral interest to logical positivists. Babbitt's claims of significance rested instead on an unspoken syllogism that combined historical valuation with technical progress: (1) Schoenberg was a significant composer who had developed a revolutionary method of composition; (2) Babbitt systematized and generalized the method; (3) therefore, Babbitt inherited Schoenberg's significance.

The argument did not convince me. Babbitt's translation of Schoenberg's culturally situated serial practice into abstract operations along multiple musical dimensions was a huge leap that shed aesthetic interest and perceptual coherence. Nor could I believe in the idea that

1. See Babbitt 2003, 78–85.

artistic significance depended on historical inheritance and innovation. Was Schoenberg a great composer because he took necessary historical steps in the evolution of tonality and post-tonality? Schoenberg may have thought so, but I did not. For me, Schoenberg's music stood or fell on its own merits. I denied the historical necessity and significance of Babbitt's system and resultant music. Yet I too became a composer-theorist, albeit of a different kind. Sometimes our greatest influences come from those we reject. Babbitt's influence on me was twofold: on the negative side, an awareness of how I did not want music to be; on the positive side, a powerful example of thinking music through, boldly and systematically, from the bottom up.

In my compositional crisis I felt cornered in two ways. On the one hand, there were diverse and largely incompatible musical styles to choose from, yet I found none to be compelling. The existence of many possibilities brought not only confusion but also a sense that the arrow of history was lost. Any choice of how to proceed seemed arbitrary. On the other hand, the most prestigious styles employed compositional methods that were opaque to perception; that is, these methods had only an indirect relation to how listeners construed the resulting music.[2] This was true not only of Babbitt but also, in differing degrees, of Boulez, Stockhausen, and Carter. An anecdote will clarify the point. I attended a rehearsal in which Babbitt coached one of his pieces.[3] A prominent E♭ octave sounded, and the performers asked him if one of the instruments should play E♮. He could not supply the answer until he consulted his row chart. Even he, with his acute musical hearing and elitist claims to musical expertise, did not know by ear which note was required. Can you imagine Mozart or Brahms in that predicament?

The phenomena of incompatible styles and opaque compositional methods were related. When a compositional method is inaccessible to perception, it does not easily spread in common usage but tends to be

---

2. I developed this point at some length in the article "Cognitive Constraints on Compositional Systems" (Lerdahl 1988a). See chapter 4 for further discussion.

3. *All Set,* rehearsed at Baruch College in New York City in 1976.

private and idiosyncratic. Moreover, given the high value assigned to novelty within the prevailing modernist aesthetic, the invention of a new private method could be considered more important than the artistic result.

I found this situation insupportable and sought a different way forward. I had no idea how to proceed until, in 1970, I read Noam Chomsky's *Language and Mind* (Chomsky 1968), which advanced the hypothesis that beneath the variety of languages lies an abstract core that all languages share and, further, that the language capacity could be studied scientifically by developing rule systems and comparing the output of rules against linguistic data. If this approach was possible for language, why could it not be for music? I imagined a way to transcend the splintering of musical styles that surrounded me and to clear my mind of the dubious notion that composer Y was significant by taking the next step from composer X, and so on in a line of supposed historical progress. Instead of looking to predecessors whom I regarded as problematic as a guide for how to compose, I would seek to understand the musical mind itself and base my composing on that. This understanding would help develop a perceptually transparent compositional method. I moved to the Boston area, the center of generative linguistics, where I hoped to find a linguist with whom to collaborate in building a comprehensive theoretical edifice.

I can now place these ambitions in a wider context. Other composers around 1970 were also rejecting hidden compositional methods and searching for organizational means that were accessible to perception. One thinks of the minimalists and Steve Reich's statement that his interest was "in a compositional process and a sounding music that are one and the same thing" (Reich 2004, 35). A few years later, a similar impulse led the spectralists Gérard Grisey and Tristan Murail to try to build musical form directly from the acoustic features of sound.

More broadly, many in my generation found it difficult to believe any longer in a clear historical narrative. Leonard Meyer, in his prescient book *Music, the Arts, and Ideas,* argued that art was entering a phase of mutually incompatible styles that would remain in stasis (Meyer 1967, 89–232). This development was a consequence of the availability of art from all times and cultures and of the resulting dispersion of cultural authority. The habitual experimentation characteristic of modernist composition contributed to this dispersion, for individual artists pursued novelty in individual ways, leading to conflicting claims for the future and hence to a sense that everything had become relative and contingent. Furthermore, the old avant-garde had found its direction and energy by taking previously forbidden stylistic steps, but after Cage there were no more rules to break. Anything was possible. The loss of historical narrative caused a variety of postmodern reactions. Some responded with irony and pastiche; others sought comfort in the past, often through quotation; others persisted in pursuit of a private utopia; still others transferred the appetite for artistic experimentation to technological innovation. Among composers, as far as I know, only Leonard Bernstein and I turned seriously to generative linguistics for enlightenment.

I am referring, of course, to Bernstein's well-known Norton Lectures at Harvard, published later as *The Unanswered Question* (Bernstein 1976). Bernstein's and my goals were different. He appealed to hypotheses about the innateness of the language capacity to justify the tonality that he had employed in his greatest successes as a composer, and he supported his argument with literal analogies between language and music. I had a more open agenda: to adopt some of linguistic methodology, rather than specific analogies, in order to begin to formulate a substantive theory of the musical mind. I wanted to make new things with what I hoped to find. Contrasting attitudes aside, Bernstein's appearance at Harvard was fortunate, for his talks gave rise to heated debates in the community, and through these I met the collaborator I was seeking, the linguist Ray Jackendoff. It was to Bernstein that we made our first presentation in a small gathering at Harvard's Eliot House.

I had already encountered Bernstein in 1972 at Tanglewood, not long before his lectures. I was there for the premiere of my first major orchestral piece. Still in the throes of a creative crisis, I took the extreme step of basing the piece entirely on the notes of the B♭ major triad, as a placeholder so as to shift the locus of interest from pitch, the organization of which I was struggling with in vain, onto an intricate display of rhythm and color. On arriving at Tanglewood, I went to the weekly composition seminar and found myself face to face with Bernstein and Carter, neither of whom I had yet met. They were visibly uncomfortable with each other, as anyone familiar with the musical politics of the time can imagine, and seized on the distraction of my strange score, poring over it in spirited conversation. This exercise relieved their tension if not mine.

That year the composer and conductor Bruno Maderna substituted for Gunther Schuller as director of Tanglewood's contemporary music festival. A modernist centrist, he had no sympathy for my experiment and cancelled the performance after a few rehearsals, causing a small fracas in the press. The next winter, Schuller met with me to say that since I wrote the piece, he was determined to perform it. I have always been grateful to him for that. By that point, however, I was no longer satisfied with just a major triad and replied that I wanted to rewrite the piece with all 12 notes. I renamed it *Chords*. Schuller premiered it at Tanglewood on August 8, 1974, an unforgettable date because on that evening Richard Nixon resigned his presidency following the Watergate scandal. Almost everyone stayed home to watch the resignation on television. Those few who attended the concert heard Nixon's speech over loudspeakers, followed directly by a rather dazed premiere of *Chords*.

This series of mishaps proved to be the turning point in my quest as composer and musical thinker. The sudden appearance of a major triad in my music revealed to me that I wanted my music to have tonal centers. A B♭ major triad by itself, however, is a center only in a primitive sense. What was needed was both a center and degrees of distance from it, so that the music could depart and return, tense and relax; further, it must be possible to establish subsidiary centers. The experience also told me

Figure 1.2. Chord-color rhythms at the beginning of *Chords*.

that I wanted harmonies with degrees of psychoacoustic rootedness, from the clear root of a major triad to an ambiguous or effectively nonexistent root. Moreover, I wanted to escape the grayness of constant circulation of the chromatic aggregate by having at my disposal a full palette of harmonies, from a simple triad to a 12-note sonority. Finally, I wanted to endow rhythm and timbre with structural rather than merely impressionistic value. All of these ideas later found a place in my theories.

Figure 1.2 gives the opening of *Chords,* a gradual transition from a B♭ major triad to a dissonant hexachord, developed with subtly syncopated rhythms against shifting color-chords of three flutes, then three violas, three clarinets, three cellos, and so on. This mosaiclike conception is anti-orchestral in its demands, for each instrumental group must find its exact rhythmic place as a phrase unfolds, more or less as in Central African ensemble music (Arom 1991). The succession of harmonies and timbres, however, proceeds without clear organization (although there are hints of the chromatic neighbor notes and equal divisions of the octave that emerged in subsequent works).[4]

Figure 1.3 shows the climax of *Chords*, a tutti arrival on an incomplete B♭ major triad—as the composer Seymour Shifrin remarked to me, like a big ship coming to dock after a perilous voyage. The B♭ harmony

4. In 2018, I revised *Chords* in an arrangement for thirteen instruments, changing many details and making it more feasible to perform. What this version loses in sonic richness it gains in rhythmic and polyphonic clarity.

Figure 1.3. Climax of *Chords.*

piles up into a 12-note chord, recapitulating in foreshortened form the progression in figure 1.2 from triad to chromatic dissonance.

The opening of Grisey's *Partiels,* composed a year later, shares with *Chords* the reintroduction into contemporary music of psychoacoustic consonance and harmonic rootedness. The alleged imperatives of history, however, later drove the spectral movement into higher overtones and inharmonic spectra in order to avoid association with past tonal practice (exceptions are the music of Claude Vivier and Georg Friedrich Haas). This is the contradiction at the heart of spectralism: to base harmony on the harmonic series and then cover it up. The view of musical progress as an unwavering march from consonance to dissonance has always struck me as simplistic. From *Chords* onward, my music engaged with a full range of consonance and dissonance and degrees of tonal centricity and noncentricity. An inclusive view of harmony and centricity offered a world of structural and expressive possibilities that I had no wish to renounce.

Such a view does not shun past practice. Contemporary European composers tend to feel the weight of the past and flee from it. In a high modernist aesthetic, any association with earlier or popular practice is frowned on. Early modernists did not feel that way. Debussy evoked all kinds of music, Stravinsky and Bartók thrived on transmutation of folk materials, and Schoenberg synthesized old and new in his mature style. American composers, in contrast to their European contemporaries, are relatively free of the burden of history. I have gladly embraced the past as well as the future. To put it another way, these categories of time have not controlled my musical thought. Nor has the imitation of past styles, as in the neo-Romanticism that emerged around the time of *Chords* in the music of George Rochberg and David Del Tredici, interested me. I saw no reason to repeat less well what others had done before. My embrace of the past—and the future—could only be on my terms, in my own musical idiom.

I have always had an affinity for music theory. In my first year of college in 1962, while studying sixteenth-century counterpoint, I read Thomas Mann's *Doctor Faustus,* with its Adorno-drenched brew of hidden artistic order and social diagnosis.[5] Like Adrian Leverkühn, the antihero of the novel, I tried my hand at 12-tone composition, but I was repelled by the kind of constraints that the method imposed. The serial method is a permutational system (Babbitt 2003, 56). A given row prescribes a specific interval-class order, and the canonical 12-tone operations preserve that order while permuting the pitch classes of the aggregate. Take, for example, the opening six notes of the melody of Schoenberg's Fourth Quartet in figure 1.4a. These can be transposed, inverted, or reversed. But it is contrary to the spirit of the system (albeit not impossible within it) to embellish the melody freely, as in figure

5. Theodor Wiesengrund Adorno was Mann's musical advisor for *Doctor Faustus;* see Mann 1961.

Figure 1.4. Opening theme of Schoenberg's Fourth String Quartet:
(a) the original, (b) elaboration of the theme, (c) simplification of
the theme.

1.4b, or simplify it, as in figure 1.4c, for these steps violate the order of
interval classes. While doing Palestrina-style counterpoint exercises, I
enjoyed finding ways of embellishing contrapuntal lines within a structural framework. Most music from around the world, be it Indian raga,
Japanese koto, or American jazz, thrives on embellishment. The syntax
of human languages is structured similarly: one can elaborate a subject
and verb at will with adjectives, adverbs, prepositional phrases, and
subordinate clauses. When studying counterpoint, I had not yet even
heard of Heinrich Schenker, but I instinctively sought an elaborational
syntax, a hierarchy of structure and ornament. The distinction between
permutational and elaborational systems was my first important theoretical insight. The concept of hierarchical elaboration eventually
became fundamental to my work in composition and theory.

Later, while in graduate school at Princeton, I immersed myself in
Schoenberg's preserial music in search of an alternative to the 12-tone
path. One reason I did so was a dislike of the binary division of music
into tonal and atonal. The prevailing attitude was that Schenker
explained tonal music and Babbitt explained 12-tone music. On the
horizon was pitch-class set theory (Forte 1973), which addressed preserial atonal music by principles unlike those that explain tonal music.
No one granted continuity between tonal and atonal. I sought to forge
this, to me, evident continuity, for I loved the so-called transitional

music of Debussy and Schoenberg, and I admired Bartók's unique synthesis of Classical, folk, and modernist materials. I undertook an ambitious essay that attempted to establish an evolution rather than a rupture between tonal and atonal, focusing on Schoenberg's early development. I gave it up because I lacked adequate theoretical tools. Many years later some of this material appeared in a theoretically well-developed context in my book *Tonal Pitch Space* (hereafter referred to as TPS) (Lerdahl 2001b, chapter 7). But at the time I needed help to become a theorist.

Jackendoff and I began our theoretical collaboration in earnest soon after I finished *Chords*. We saw our enterprise as a branch of the emerging interdisciplinary field of cognitive science. Our goal was to take as input a musical surface—that is, a sequence of pitches and rhythms, leaving aside the psychoacoustic construction of these musical objects— and yield as output the heard structure that a listener unconsciously infers from the input. The heart of the theory would be a set of psychologically motivated rules that predicts output from input. The emerging theory was eventually published as *A Generative Theory of Tonal Music* (hereafter GTTM) (Lerdahl and Jackendoff 1983).

When in one of my theoretical phases, I have pursued ideas and formalizations for their own sake and often in enormous detail, and on a few occasions I have enjoyed productive collaborations with experimental psychologists in testing the theory (Bigand, Parncutt, and Lerdahl 1996; Lerdahl and Krumhansl 2007). These efforts have sometimes taken me far from composition. Yet the theoretical work has always informed my music, sometimes well in advance of a precise theoretical formulation. The influence has been mutual: theory feeds composition, and composing gives rise to theoretical ideas.

GTTM and TPS have multiple analytic components, each with its own rule system. Implicitly at work in *Chords* were the rhythmic components of grouping and meter and the pitch-domain components of sensory dissonance and pitch space. Sensory—that is, psychoacoustic— dissonance is the perceptual backdrop against which a given musical syntax treats musical dissonance. Pitch space quantifies the cognitive distance of pitches, chords, and keys from one another within a given idiom. Years later, in TPS, I developed these pitch-domain components in theoretical terms. By contrast, it is difficult to find traces in *Chords* of the time-span and prolongational components that Jackendoff and I were soon to develop for GTTM. I did not yet have a clear understanding of the principle of elaboration.

By 1975 Jackendoff and I were making progress on the theory of event hierarchies, and I immediately applied this work to my music. *Eros* (1975), for mezzo-soprano and chamber ensemble, is cast as a continuous set of twenty-one Classical variations, each twenty bars long. I chose variation form because it directly exploits the elaborative nature of music. *Eros* also evokes North India raga, another genre that clearly projects structural and ornamental pitches. In addition, *Eros* implicitly incorporates the component of tonal attraction, which addresses the yearning of unstable pitches to anchor on nearby stable pitches (Bharucha 1984a). My intuitive conception of attractions was of a force field of tugs and pulls on a melodic line. Again, the theoretical formulation of this intuition waited many years until TPS was written.

To describe this point further, I must introduce the tree notation employed in GTTM and TPS. Suppose that two events x and y are hierarchically connected as in figure 1.5. In condition (a), the right branch to y is subordinate to the branch to x, signifying that y elaborates x. The reverse holds in condition (b), with x as a left branch to y. Moreover, a right branch signifies a tensing motion as in (a), and a left branch signifies a relaxing motion as in (b). From a temporal perspective, in (a) y is heard retrospectively in relation to x; in (b) x is heard prospectively in relation to y. In phenomenological terms (Husserl 1964), right branching denotes retention and depends on memory; left branching denotes protention and relies on expectation.

Figure 1.6 shows the first phrase of *Eros* with its *alap*-like drone and ornamented melody. Above the melody is a hierarchical analysis employing both the tree notation and an equivalent slur notation. (The

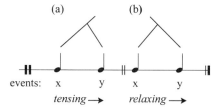

(a)   (b)

events: x   y   x   y

tensing →   *relaxing* →

Figure 1.5. Tree notation for hierarchical event structures.

dashed branch to the E♭ indicates an alternative connection when shifting from right to left branching.) The basic structural motion, indicated by the highest branching, is from A to D, which dominates the progression as the tonal center. Within this framework, the tree describes two wavelets of tension-relaxation, the first one relaxing into A, the second tensing away from A and relaxing into D. The salient point is double leading-tone motion, first G♯ and B♭ to A and then E♭ and C♯ to D. The idea of double leading tones came from the unfinished study of Schoenberg's transitional music from chromatic tonality into atonality. These half-step tendency tones, whether resolved or not, project strong attractions. Their use in *Eros* is pervasive, as befits its subject matter. To adapt phraseology from Schopenhauer and Schenker, desire transmutes into the will of the tones.

After the opening variation with its drone pedal, subsequent variations build on a ground bass comprised of pitches that divide the octave equally into minor and then major thirds, with each pitch having a precise time-point location. The leading-tone constructions in the melody, the rigorous bass line, and the fixed length of each variation combined to create, for the first time in my music, a work in which many elements took a logical place. Formal rigor is only one kind of aesthetic goal, yet it is one to which I have periodically returned. But there were reasons not to be fully satisfied with the formal gains achieved in *Eros*. Melody and bass were essentially unrelated and did not produce a coherent syntax of harmonic progression. The variation form was too derivative of Classical models to be relied on for long. Elaborative

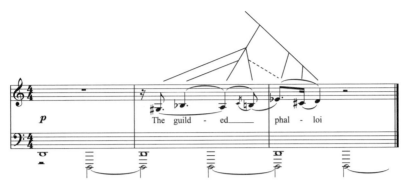

Figure 1.6. *Eros*, first phrase with its hierarchical analysis.

treatment within a variation bore little connection to the global form of twenty-one sequential variations.

First I tackled the issue of harmonic progression. Double-leading tones to the tonic and dominant pitches can be realized not only horizontally but also vertically, turning the voice leading in figure 1.7a into the harmonic progression in figure 1.7b. The lower C, notated in parentheses, displaces the resolution to G in the lower voice so that the final sonority is in root position. This progression acts like a dominant-to-tonic progression in the sense that the most proximate chord resolves on the tonic. Proximity is realized, however, not as bass motion by fifth supporting diatonic stepwise motion but as bass motion by tritone supporting four-way chromatic stepwise motion. Unlike the standard tonal case, the chord types are different: not two triads but a chord of stacked fourths (respelled enharmonically) resolving to an open fifth. The sense of resolution is driven by the psychoacoustics—that is, from moderate sensory dissonance to sensory consonance. Figure 1.7c inserts a third chord at the left through voice leading again by semitone. I used this three-stage progression in one piece but was not satisfied because the first chord is more consonant than the second. Replacing the first chord in figure 1.7c by pitches a whole step away produces figure 1.7d. Now there is an orderly progression from dissonance to consonance: very

Figure 1.7. Elements of a harmonic and voice-leading syntax.

dissonant tritones and semitones to moderately dissonant stacked fourths to a fully consonant fifth. This progression provides clear movement from tension to relaxation and thus serves the role of closure.

The voice leading in figure 1.7d is symmetrical, yet it is based on the asymmetry of the division of the octave into a fifth and a fourth. My music often displays an inclination for near symmetries, in the time domain as well as in musical space. More central from a cognitive standpoint, however, are the two factors behind the progression: the principle of tonal attraction, caused by relative proximity and stability, and the incorporation of sensory dissonance as a driver of harmonic syntax.

Having addressed voice-leading and harmonic issues, I next considered formal issues. While developing the theory of event hierarchies with Jackendoff, I had worked through many analyses of tonal pieces, stripping away ornamental pitches and chords from level to level systematically by rule, until an underlying skeleton of structural events was reached, ultimately the tonic chord. It struck me that I could reverse the process in my own music by starting with a kernel element and elaborating it in successive steps. Vertical levels of a hierarchy would string out sequentially. The result would be a kind of variation form, not variations of fixed length as in Classical music but geometrically expanding variations—or, as I often call it, spiral form. This modus operandi unites local voice-leading procedures and global form under one principle, that of elaboration.

I initially fulfilled these ideas in the First String Quartet (1978). Its beginning in figure 1.8 lays out expanding variations in an almost

Figure 1.8. First String Quartet, beginning.

deadpan pedagogical manner, *sempre piano* and *non vibrato*. A bracket marks each variation. Variation 1 presents notes of the harmonic series on bass G. Variation 2 prolongs the opening sonority. Variations 3 and 4 assemble the cadential closure shown in figure 1.7d, transposed to G. Variation 5 modulates the progression to C♯, which is the bass and root of the stacked-fourth chord, and returns to the tonic G in a less stable melodic position, followed by closure. Variation 6 further elaborates this progression and begins to assert the independence of individual lines.

Figure 1.9 represents the prolongational hierarchy of the beginning of the First Quartet by the slur and tree notations employed in the co-evolving music theory. (Dashed slurs connect identical pitch classes.) The

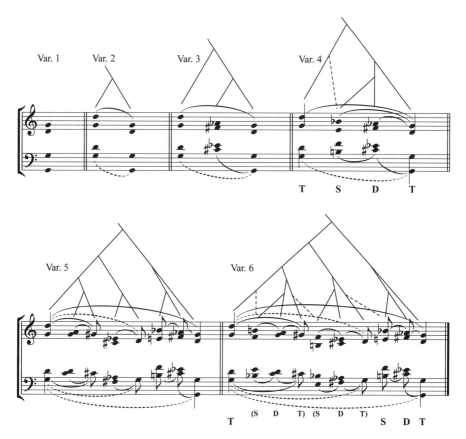

Figure 1.9. Structural analysis of the beginning of the First Quartet.

rhythmic grouping of events in the music reinforces these branching units. In Variation 4, the function categories T, D, and S are given beneath the music. Function markings continue in Variations 5 and 6 to show embedded functions in relation to C♯ and then back to G. These do not mean "tonic," "dominant," and "subdominant" in a traditional Riemannian sense (Riemann 1893); I could just as well say "function 1," "function 2," and "function 3." The categories represent functional role as a consequence of hierarchical position. I articulated this theory of functionality later in TPS, but already I was intuitively incorporating it in my music.

The syntax of the First Quartet employs in one way or another most of GTTM's and TPS's components. The most interesting difference is in how its treatment of pitch space and tension differs from how the tonal theory developed. In my music, sensory dissonance plays a major syntactic role, whereas it has only a surface role in Classical tonal syntax. Once passing and neighboring tones and suspensions are stripped away in Classical music, every chord is a triad. The diatonic tonal system projects patterns of tension and relaxation less through sensory dissonance than by a multidimensional geometry of chord and key distances.

In the history of Western music, the incorporation of sensory dissonance at deeper than surface levels of syntax was a feature of music in Machaut's time, but by Josquin it largely disappeared until the mid-nineteenth century. It resumed with the opposition in Wagner's music between diatonic and chromatic domains. Think, for instance, of the harmonic contrast between day and night in *Tristan und Isolde* or between holiness and sin in *Parsifal*. Debussy intensified this trend through the introduction of exotic scales and sonorities, and Schoenberg incorporated it explicitly in his Chamber Symphony, op. 9, in which the progression from fourth chord to whole-tone chord to triad, or the reverse, dominates much of the discourse. One finds this trend also in Bartók and Messiaen. (For related discussion, see Lerdahl 2001b, 317–20.) A thorough if flawed statement of this way of thinking appeared in Hindemith ([1937] 1942). Whatever one may think of Hindemith as a composer, as a theorist he was quite suggestive.

On comparing myself to my predecessors and contemporaries, my music stands out in at least one important way. I refer here not to originality or "voice," as Aaron Copland used to put it, although I always had that, but to my ambition to develop a complex yet intelligible syntax. Not for me were the perceptually inaccessible complications of postwar serialism, the simplicities of minimalism, the derivative nostalgia of neo-Romanticism, or spectralism's immersion in unstructured, sensuous tone color. I have aimed for a kind of musical syntax in all the musical dimensions that is accessible to perception yet capable of developing into great complexity.

When composing the opening of the First Quartet, I had two concrete models in mind: the pure sound of Purcell's viol fantasias, and Wagner's evocations of the creation of an entire imaginary world at the beginnings of *Rheingold* and *Tristan*. It seemed advisable to build the foundation of an imaginary world from simple elements that could support a variety of multifaceted superstructures without crumbling. In the initial pages of the First Quartet I found such a foundation, and with it I announced, quietly but firmly, a fresh beginning.

CHAPTER TWO

Genesis and Architecture of the Music Theory

Jackendoff and I began our theoretical project from a linguistic perspective but without any intent to treat music as a language. It was less the specifics of generative linguistics than Chomsky's general way of framing issues that attracted us: the supposition of specialized mental capacities, the belief that they could be studied rigorously by investigating the structure of their outputs, the distinction between an idealized capacity and its external and often accidental manifestations, the idea of a limited set of principles or rules that could generate a potentially infinite set of outputs, and the possibility that some of these principles might be unvarying beneath a capacity's many different cultural manifestations (Chomsky 1965).

To make this vision concrete for music, we decided to focus on a particular musical idiom yet with a view to how particular formulations might be generalized. We chose Classical tonal music because it was an idiom we shared. Moreover, it was already a well-theorized idiom, so we did not have to begin from scratch. In keeping with the American music-theoretic climate in the 1970s, we turned to Schenker's analytic system, which in its final and most influential incarnation (Schenker 1935) could be viewed as a protogenerative theory. Schenker posited an originating structure for all tonal music, the *Ursatz* (funda-

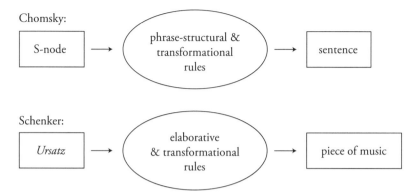

Figure 2.1. Analogy between (early) Chomskian and Schenkerian theories. Rectangles signify structures, ellipses rules.

mental structure), which comprises a I-V-I harmonic elaboration of the tonic triad supporting a stepwise melodic descent to the tonic. From this structure he developed, through stages of hierarchical elaboration and transformation, successive structural levels until a musical surface, or piece of music, was reached. The same elaborative and transformational principles applied recursively from level to level. These structural levels and transformations could be interpreted from a late twentieth-century perspective as representing cognitive structures and operations. The form of his theory seemed comparable to Chomsky's generative method from S-node ("sentence node," or top level of the phrase-structure hierarchy) through phrase-structural and transformational rules to surface structure. Figure 2.1 summarizes the parallel. Schenker's writings, however, were informal. It seemed a logical first step to formalize his methodology.[1]

For several reasons, we soon gave up this Chomskian-Schenkerian approach. First, we could not justify the *Ursatz*. Although this a priori

1. As far as I know, Milton Babbitt's student Michael Kassler (1963) was the first to try to cast Schenkerian theory as a propositional analytic system. Martin Rohrmeier (2011) has resumed the idea a generative production model of tonal music through a deft blend of Riemannian function theory with Schenkerian hierarchical theory.

construct was understandably central for Schenker, a thinker steeped in nineteenth-century German philosophical idealism, its status made little sense to a modern, scientifically inclined American. Nor could schema theory in cognitive psychology (Neisser 1967) defend this construct, for the *Ursatz* is too remote from a musical surface to be picked up and organized by a listener who is not already predisposed to find it. Second, the *Ursatz* is inapplicable to music of other times and cultures. We sought a theoretical framework that could accommodate diverse musical idioms. Third, the nonrhythmic character of the *Ursatz* presented a formal and musical problem. How was rhythm to be introduced into the derivation, and why should it have inferior status? Fourth, even supposing that the *Ursatz* or some comparable structure could be justified as a foundation, there would be many possible ways of generating a given musical surface. How could derivations be constrained? Fifth and most importantly, what of psychological interest would there be even if we managed to build a system that generated this or that piece from an *Ursatz*-like foundation? What mattered to us was not the output per se but the structure attributed to the output. It was not clear how generating a piece could reveal much about mental structures and their principles of organization.

Reflecting on these considerations, we decided to formulate our theory in the opposite way. Rather than begin with a putative ideal structure and generate musical surfaces, we would begin with musical surfaces and generate their structural descriptions, as shown in figure 2.2. There would be no hypothetical point of origin oriented toward a particular musical style, no systemic elevation of pitch over rhythm, and no problem of exploding derivations. We could work directly with music that we found of interest and value. The rules would be motivated psychologically and would represent cognitive principles of organization. The structural descriptions would correspond to predicted heard structures. The theory would be testable.

Empirically oriented theories simplify phenomena in order to make an investigation manageable. Four methodological assumptions or ide-

Figure 2.2. Overall form of the GTTM theory.

alizations, largely adapted from generative linguistics, helped launch our enterprise. We assumed:

(1) a musical surface—pitches and rhythms—ignoring the complex psychoacoustic processes by which these musical objects are constructed perceptually;

(2) a single sequence of events, collapsing contrapuntal strands into a single stream;

(3) a generic listener familiar with a musical style through sufficient exposure and with implicit knowledge of that style;

(4) a final-state representation, setting aside the difficult problem of how the listener processes structure in real time.

The first two idealizations were tactical simplifications. The study of the conversion of sound into musical objects belongs to the fields of signal processing, psychoacoustics, and now neuroscience. Music theories have generally taken pitches and rhythms as their starting point. However, what constitutes a musical object is a complicated question, especially in contemporary music, so ultimately there should be a convergence between the two levels of inquiry. The second idealization was conceived of as a temporary convenience. Subsequently, Lerdahl (2001b, 32–34) sketched how multiple streams can be treated within the theory.

The remaining idealizations—implicit learning by exposure and final-state representation of knowledge—are familiar in cognitive science. Concerning the latter, we felt that it would be advantageous to specify the mental structures in question before trying to articulate how they operate in real time. This idealization has led to misunderstanding, for instance in the claim that I postulate "lossless [*sic*] musical perception" (Tymoczko

2011, 26). I am as aware as anyone of processing errors, memory limitations, and general variability in musical listening. The final-state idealization permits one to disregard such factors in order to search undeterred for organizing principles and structures. Once principles and structures are reasonably well understood, it is easier to address processing issues.

These idealizations were not meant to denigrate psychoacoustics or processing. They were strategic decisions in theory construction. They also had the advantage of keeping our project within the bounds of the music-theory tradition, since most music theories take pitches and rhythms for granted, appeal to intuitive plausibility, and do not restrict the study of musical works to their real-time unfolding.

In launching our project, we took notice of Meyer's (1973, 44–105) distinction between hierarchical and associative structures (for the latter he used the term *conformant*). Hierarchical structures concern the domination and subordination of events to one another. Associative structures concern the degree of relatedness of events or of groups of events. Motivic relations are usually thought of as associative: motive A is similar or dissimilar to motive B, but neither dominates the other. Likewise, timbral relations are typically seen as associative: a trumpet sounds more like a trombone than a viola, but these relations do not involve domination or subordination.

Associative relations are difficult to formalize, and they often rely on hierarchical features. We decided to restrict our project to hierarchies and began to develop rules to assign hierarchical structure to pitch events. The idea, as in figure 2.3, was to articulate stability conditions that decide the relative hierarchical importance of events—the more stable the event, the higher its position in the hierarchy. From Schenkerian theory we loosely adapted the term *prolongational reduction* to signify hierarchically related pitch connections.[2] We adapted tree struc-

---

2. In a music-theoretic context, the term *prolongation* essentially means elaboration: a neighboring note or chord elaborates and prolongs a given note or chord, and a piece elaborates and prolongs the tonic. The term *reduction* means hierarchy: subordinate events are *reduced out*.

Figure 2.3. Beginnings of a model of hierarchical pitch-event structures.

tures from linguistic theory to represent prolongational structures, but there was no attempt to seek analogues to parts of speech or syntactic phrases. Rather, as described in chapter 1 (figure 1.8), trees denoted elaborative relations between events in an expanded sense of ordinary melodic/harmonic embellishment.

This initial attempt foundered on two related grounds. First, the theory did not specify which events to compare for connections. Events could hardly branch indiscriminately. The theory required nested regions of analysis. Second, events repeat, often identically or nearly so. Schubert's *Moment Musical*, no. 6, given in figure 2.4, will illustrate. A tonic root-position A♭ major chord with melodic C takes place in the pickup to bar 1 and in bars 5, 8, 47, 53, 58, 61, and 63. How might the theory assign each such occurrence its proper structural importance and prolongational connection? From many such cases, it became apparent that neither the importance of an event nor how it related to other events could be separated from its position in the temporal order. We could not build a rule system to assign a hierarchy of events without developing a theory of rhythm.

The prevailing attitude in the 1970s was that pitch was well understood but rhythm was intractable. Nevertheless, some writers theorized about rhythm, either in terms of quasi-metrical groupings (Cooper and Meyer 1960; Cone 1968) or metrically oriented pitch reduction (Komar 1971; Lewin [1974] 2013; Schachter 1980; Westergaard 1975). We reviewed these approaches and forged solutions to problems that beset them. The key was to disentangle grouping and meter from each other and treat them as independent components. The grouping component parses a musical surface hierarchically into subphrases, phrases, and sections. The metrical component describes hierarchical patterns of strong and weak beats.

Figure 2.4. Schubert, *Moment Musical,* no. 6 (Trio omitted).

Figure 2.5 gives the grouping and metrical structures for the first phrase of the Schubert. Grouping structure is established at multiple levels by a combination of local principles of proximity and similarity and global principles of symmetry and parallelism. The grouping, shown by brackets beneath the music, projects a typical musical sentence (*Satz*): two bars of statement, two of counterstatement, and four of continuation and cadence. GTTM's grouping component is concerned only with the establishment of groupings and does not label them. Chapter 5 in TPS,

Figure 2.4. *continued*

however, takes the additional step of labeling groupings through its sub-
theory of functionality. Here I follow TPS's practice.

Above the grouping brackets in figure 2.5 is a metrical grid. Each row of
dots represents a level of conceptually isochronous beats. The note value
at the left of each row signifies the notational duration from one beat to
the next in that row. If a beat is perceived to be strong at one level, it is also

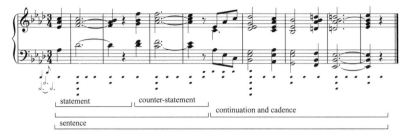

Figure 2.5. Grouping structure and metrical grid of the first phrase of the *Moment Musical*.

a beat at the next larger level. This is the sense in which metrical structure is hierarchical. Most musical styles have a limited repertoire of grids. The listener establishes a particular grid by finding the best fit between an available grid and the pattern of stresses at the musical surface. The meter for the phrase is straightforward: duple meter at the eighth-note level in bar 4; triple meter throughout at the quarter-note level; and duple meter at hypermetrical levels (levels larger than the notated meter).

These two components describe different mental constructs. Grouping represents stretches of chunked musical time; meter represents inferred beats at points in time. Grouping boundaries and beat periodicities may or may not be in phase. Here they are slightly out of phase, for each group begins with a quarter-note upbeat to the next bar.

Investigation of the grouping component brought us to Gestalt psychology with its extensive literature on visual grouping (Koffka 1935). It was unclear how to make a musical grammar out of the gestalt principles of proximity and similarity. Working through many grouping and metrical analyses, we found that the phenomena were a matter of degree rather than categorical. If different factors converged on the same result, a grouping or metrical intuition was strong. If they conflicted, the intuition was weak or ambiguous. Standard linguistic grammars, in contrast, yielded *yes* or *no* grammatical results; there were no shades of gray. Soon we concluded that perceptual judgments were gradual not only for grouping and meter but also for other aspects of musical structure. We decided to overhaul the rule system that we were developing. Well-formedness rules defined possible hierarchical features and replaced the role of recursive phrase-structure rules, which as a rule type we had imported from linguistic theory. Transformational rules, which were then central to generative linguistics, were demoted to handle marginal cases such as grouping overlap and metrical deletion. We put front and center a new kind of system, preference rules, whose purpose was to select from the many possible well-formed descriptions those few that best matched, in gradient fashion, intuitions in response to a given musical surface.

The first phrase of the Schubert does not project grouping or metrical ambiguities; the preference rules that derive these structures converge on single results. The case is more complex in the middle section of the piece. Bars 17–24 continue the previous eight-bar grouping and metrical pattern, but the answering phrase in bars 25–33 is nine bars long (4 + 5 instead of 4 + 4). As a result, the cadence in bar 33 seems to end, by metrical inertia, on a hypermetrical downbeat, as shown in figure 2.6a. The phrase extensions in bars 34–36 and 37–39 are each three bars in duration, yielding a temporary three-bar hypermetrical pattern, and the accented diminished-seventh chords in bars 34 and 37 appear on hypermetrical weak beats. The music reverts to the initial four-bar hypermetrical pattern in bar 42. A consequence of this interpretation is that throughout the passage the grouping and metrical structures are acutely out of phase; that is, hypermetrical strong beats do not begin near the beginnings of groups. This is not a preferred outcome. Figure 2.6b gives an alternative interpretation in which the cadence at bar 33 adjusts to take place on a weak hypermetrical beat and the diminished-seventh chords are on hypermetrical downbeats. Now grouping and meter are virtually in phase. This is the somewhat preferred analysis in an ambiguous context.

When GTTM was published, preference rules were criticized for not behaving in proper grammatical fashion (Peel and Slawson 1984). They were seen as insufficiently quantified. While true, this was not an objection in principle. GTTM avoids the intricacies of rule quantification in order to concentrate on the musical and cognitive principles at

Figure 2.6. Two hypermetrical interpretations for the middle portion of the *Moment Musical*.

hand. Our formal goal was not full quantification, which could come later, but enough precision for the proposed components and rules to be investigated empirically.[3]

A deeper objection was that preference rules did not assign structure through a cycle of derivational steps. In retrospect, however, the convergent rather than derivational character of preference rules turned out to be a pioneering aspect of what is now a common computational framework in cognitive science, whether in the form of schema theory, parametric variables with dynamic programming, neural networks, machine-learning techniques, or Bayesian probabilities. In linguistics, they show up in phonology in optimality theory (McCarthy 2001), in semantics in word meaning and categorization (Jackendoff 1983), and in syntax, at least by implication, in parametric settings of features across languages (Baker 2001). Our preference rules occupy a conceptual midpoint between neural networks, in which a given structure arises from the strongest activation in a network without reliance on rules per se, and optimality theory, in which rule derivations are ordered and ranked according to a winner-take-all principle. From our perspective, neural networks do not yield enough structure, and rule rankings rigidify the assignment of structure beyond what can be empirically justified.

The development of the grouping and metrical components not only gave rise to preference rules but also showed the way to a novel theoretical architecture. Rather than build our theory around a central component from which other components are derived, as was the case for Schenker and Chomsky, our theory took the form of several independent components that coordinate with one another to generate an overall structural description. Neither pitch nor rhythm has priority; rather, they interact.[4]

---

3. Temperley (2001, 2007) implements aspects of GTTM through dynamic programming and, later, Bayesian probabilities. Also see Hamanaka, Hirata, and Tojo 2006; Hirata and Aoyagi 2003; Marsden 2005.

4. This perspective influenced Jackendoff's subsequent work in linguistics, in which he posited that phonology, syntax, and semantics are independent systems whose structures are coordinated by interface rules. See Jackendoff 2002.

With a rhythmic theory, a rule system, and a conception of the overall architecture in hand, Jackendoff and I returned to pitch structure. A first step was to establish a single hierarchy of nested time spans so that each pitch event could have its own time-span address. A subcomponent called time-span segmentation accomplishes this step by assigning spans from beat to beat beneath the smallest grouping level but truncating metrical spans if otherwise they would cross grouping boundaries. Intuitions of upbeat and afterbeat reflect this segmentation. For example, in figure 2.6 (a or b), the first chord is an upbeat to bar 29, the third beats in bars 29–32 are afterbeats, and the triplet on beat 3 of bar 33 is an upbeat.

Ideas of rhythmic reduction, which could be traced back to Schenker (1921–24), were in the air. In particular, Lewin ([1974] 2013) systematically selected most stable events within a given metrical frame, proceeding from the bottom up but without a grouping component or treatment of cadences. The resulting shortcomings could be rectified, first by replacing metrical frames with the time-span segmentation, which combines grouping and metrical features, and second by means of cadential labeling, which preserves the structural role of cadences up to the largest level for which they function. Thus we arrived at the component of time-span reduction. Each span has a dominating event, or head, together with one or two subordinate events. The head of one span competes for dominance against another head in an equivalent span at the next larger level, and so on up to global levels.[5] The winner at any given time-span level is determined primarily by the stability conditions mentioned previously.[6]

Figure 2.7 gives the time-span reduction of local levels of the first period of the Schubert. The quarter-note level is labeled as level e. Level d retains the stable events at the measure level, and level c does

5. This way of thinking arose in part from Jackendoff's (1977) work on X-bar syntax, in which a syntactic phrase has a head that dominates other constituents in the phrase.

6. Although Lewin ([1974] 2013) influenced the development of time-span reduction, it is not the case, as Cohn (2013, 6) surmises, that Lewin's reduction criteria influenced GTTM's conception of preference rules. Jackendoff and I conceived the idea of preference rules independently in fall 1974 while incorporating gestalt principles into the grouping and metrical components that we were working on.

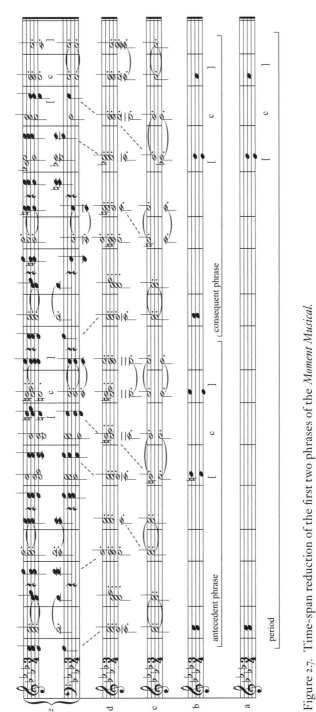

Figure 2.7. Time-span reduction of the first two phrases of the *Moment Musical*.

likewise at the two-measure level. All that remains at level b are the structural beginnings and cadences for the antecedent and consequent phrases and, at level a, the structural beginning and cadence for the period. This procedure could be continued over the entire piece.

We found that analyses generated by the time-span component were useful but insufficient. The methodology sometimes yielded unconvincing event sequences at underlying levels, and the regions of analysis were excessively tied to the rhythmic segmentation. Most critically, the analysis did not assign specific connections between events, especially nonadjacent ones such as between a tonic and its return in a reprise. We could informally draw trees and graphs that better captured the sense of prolongational reduction with which our enterprise began, but we still did not know how to derive or interpret such analyses.

Three steps enabled us to overcome this impasse. First, we recast prolongational branching as nested patterns of tonal tension and relaxation. A right branch now represented a tensing motion and a left branch a relaxing motion. This interpretation removed our thinking from the Schenkerian shadow and gave prolongational analysis a psychological flavor.[7] The second step was to give up the preconception that there ought to be just one kind of pitch reduction. We posited two kinds, time-span and prolongational, as complementary ways to understand hierarchical event structures. Time-span reduction represents the hierarchy of events in relation to the rhythmic structure, and prolongational reduction represents hierarchical patterns of tonal tension and relaxation. The third step was to derive a prolongational reduction from global to local levels of the corresponding time-span reduction via an interaction principle that acts as a rhythmic filter: if an event is in a rhythmically subordinate position, it cannot attach at global prolongational levels. Hence rhythmic position is an integral part of an event's prolongational importance. Figure 2.8 illustrates the interaction principle.

7. GTTM posits three node types for prolongational tension connections: strong prolongation for exact repetition (no increase or decrease in tension), weak prolongation for

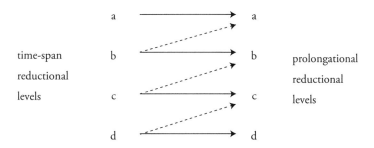

Figure 2.8. Schematic illustration of the interaction principle. A solid arrow represents a direct mapping from events in a given level of time-span reduction to an equivalent level in the associated prolongational reduction. A dashed arrow represents the access of events at a given time-span level for connection at an immediately larger prolongational level if they can connect as full repetitions.

Figure 2.9 gives the prolongational reduction derived from figure 2.7. Only the soprano and bass lines are shown. Levels are cross-labeled between the two figures. Prolongational structure is represented in two equivalent ways, by a tree and by slurs. Slurs are coextensive with branching connections. The slur notation adapts a few features from Schenkerian notation: larger note values signify more important events, and dashed slurs signify repetition of the same pitch or chord.

The slur notation is divided for readability into three staves from global to local levels. At level a, the opening tonic prolongs to the V-I cadence in bar 16. At level b, $\hat{I^3}$ at the beginning of the consequent phrase attaches to the initial $\hat{I^3}$, and the cadence of the antecedent phrase attaches as a tensing motion from the opening $\hat{I^3}$. Level c adds tonic prolongations within both phrases. The label "d→c" in the tree means that the tonic chord in bar 13 has moved from level d to level c in the prolongational reduction so that it connects directly to the tonic in bar 8, by application of the dashed-arrow condition of the interaction

_____

modified repetition (a small increase or decrease in tension), and progression for non-repetition (a relatively great increase or decrease in tension). Quantitative developments in TPS render these node distinctions superfluous, and I do not employ them here.

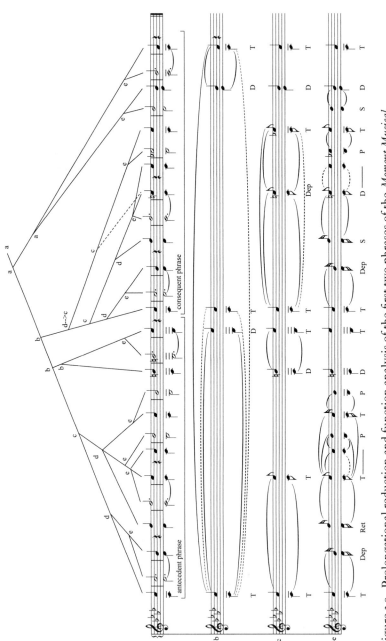

Figure 2.9. Prolongational reduction and function analysis of the first two phrases of the *Moment Musical*.

principle (see figure 2.8). The progression to V/vi in bars 10–12 is thereby contained within a tonic prolongation. Levels d–e insert the remaining elaborative details.

Beneath each staff of the slur notation in figure 2.9 is a hierarchical function analysis. My approach to functionality differs from the standard Riemannian one, for which, for instance, a IV chord always has a sub-dominant function. I distinguish between structure and function, as in the biological sciences (Lerdahl 2001b, chapter 5). A IV chord, for instance, is a structure, but its function may vary. In the cadential progression IV→V→I, it acts S, but in a I→IV→I progression at the "Amen" close of a hymn it functions as N within a tonic prolongation.[8] Its interpretation depends on its hierarchical position. Therefore TPS assigns functions—including a few more than Riemann's three basic ones—directly from the prolongational analysis. In addition, the function of an event may change depending on level. In figure 2.9, the E♭ major chord in bar 8 functions at a global level as D (V/A♭), but at more local levels it functions as T (I/E♭); that is, it is tonicized. The C major triad in bar 12 functions as Dep at a relatively global level, but locally it functions as D (V/f).[9]

Several general features of the prolongational analysis require comment. First, following the second methodological idealization listed earlier (that of a single stream of events), the graph does not differentiate between the prolongational structures of the soprano and bass lines. A Schenkerian might want, for instance, to treat the soprano in the opening I$\hat{3}$ as an initial ascent (*Anstieg*) to a more structural I$\hat{5}$ in bar 4, so that the bass A♭ in bar 1 and soprano E♭ in bar 4 align vertically at an underlying level. This transformational step can be taken at level c in figures 2.7 and 2.9—that is, at the point in the reduction where arpeggiations of the tonic chord emerge without intermediate elaborations.

---

8. Function symbols: T = tonic; D = dominant; S = subdominant (or predominant); P = passing; N = neighbor; Dep = departure; Ret = return.

9. Keys are shown in boldface, with major keys designated by large case and minor keys by small case.

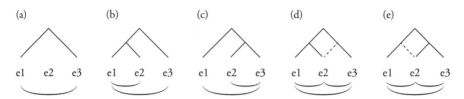

Figure 2.10. Branching constituency: (a) subordination without constituency, (b–c) subordination with constituency, (d–e) double branching to create a network-like representation.

Second, the tree notation requires that a subordinate event e2 be not merely subordinate between dominating e1 and e3, as in figure 2.10a, but that it attach as a constituent to either e1 or e3, as in figure 2.10b or c. Schenkerian analysis oscillates between constituency and nonconstituency of subordinate events. In a cadence, V typically attaches to I, as in figure 2.10c, but a neighboring or passing tone is treated as merely subordinate in its context, as in figure 2.10a. Early in the development of GTTM, Jackendoff and I considered a network formalism that would accommodate structures such as figure 2.10a, but we opted for the simpler solution of uniform strict branching (Lerdahl and Jackendoff 1983, 114–17). GTTM (183–86) justifies strict constituency (2.10b or c) by appealing to rhythmic or pitch factors that inevitably tip the balance toward either right or left branching in a given context. TPS (29–32) finesses the issue by introducing alternative dashed branches, as in 2.10d–e. This option applies not only to neighboring and passing events but also, more broadly, to contexts in which a right-branching pattern shifts to a left-branching one. This loosening of strict branching allows nonconstituent, network-like subordination under limited conditions.[10]

A third point concerns the overall method of derivation of prolongational structure. Following the fourth idealization listed above (that of

10. Yust (2015) argues cogently for a network formalism instead of a tree formalism for prolongational hierarchies. Yust (2018) extends the approach to represent meter and grouping as well as pitch-event hierarchies. The result is conceptually unifying, albeit at a cost of readability. There are many points of intersection between Yust's theory and GTTM.

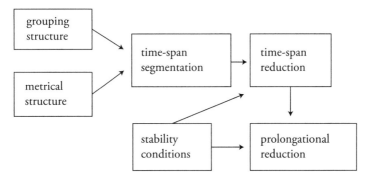

Figure 2.11. Flowchart of the main components of the GTTM theory.

a final-state theory), the interaction principle specifies a top-down derivation from a complete corresponding time-span reduction. This procedure seems counterintuitive because in the course of actual listening temporal and prolongational structures are inferred simultaneously. Jackendoff (1991) outlines how GTTM can adapt its derivations to real-time processing.[11]

As a summary of the discussion so far, the flowchart in figure 2.11 displays GTTM's components and their main connections. The stability conditions, an essential input to the time-span and prolongational reductions, have been mentioned only in passing, and indeed they are barely sketched in GTTM. After completing GTTM, I was left on my own to fill this major gap in the theory since Jackendoff quit music theory to pursue his linguistic studies. I did not know how to proceed until I encountered empirical research by Carol Krumhansl and her collaborators on the cognitive structure of tonal relations (summarized in Krumhansl 1983, 1990). One of her colleagues, Jamshed Bharucha (1984b), distinguished between event hierarchies, such as those in Schenker and GTTM, and the tonal hierarchy, by which he meant the nontemporal, schematic knowledge of the tonal system that listeners learn implicitly

11. In an otherwise different context, Katz and Pesetsky (2011) generate levels of time-span and prolongational structure together, step by step. This idea deserves exploration.

(a)   (b)

```
C                          (C)                                            A
C                G         (C)                                E     G     A
C       E        G         (C)                     C♯   E           A
C   D   E F      G    A    B (C)                   C♯ D    E F  G   A B♭
C C♯ D D♯ E F F♯ G G♯ A B♭ B (C)            C C♯ D D♯ E F F♯ G G♯ A B♭ B
```

Figure 2.12. Basic diatonic space: (a) oriented to I/**C**, (b) oriented to V⁷/**d.**

in response to exposure to a tonal idiom. It occurred to me that most of GTTM's stability conditions fit conceptually with the tonal hierarchy. If I could formalize Krumhansl's empirical data, the gap in the theory would be filled. Here was the starting point for TPS. I developed a new component for generative music theory, that of pitch space, which formalizes the schematic knowledge, beyond patterns within any particular piece, of distances among pitches, chords, and keys within the diatonic system (Lerdahl 1988b). In so doing, I introduced a type of rule absent from GTTM, that of algorithmic computation. It was possible to treat pitch space algorithmically because the tonal system itself can be viewed from a static perspective, ignoring all the interacting features in the mental representation of a particular piece. The pitch-space model strongly correlates with the empirical data and unifies the levels of pitch, chord, and key within a single framework.

The fundamental construct of the pitch-space model is the "basic space" shown in figure 2.12a, oriented to a tonic chord in C major (the actual model translates pitch names into numerical format in order to perform arithmetic operations). The space represents relationships that everyone knows intuitively: starting at the bottom row, the chromatic scale is the collection of available pitches, repeating every octave to form 12 pitch classes; the diatonic scale is built from members of the chromatic scale; the triad is built from members of the diatonic scale; the root and fifth of a triad are more stable than the third; and the root is more stable than the fifth. The basic space is an idealized form of the empirically established tone profile of pitch stability in a major key (Krumhansl and Kessler 1982).

The basic space reflects psychoacoustic consonance and dissonance. Descending by level in figure 2.12a, the octave is the most consonant interval, followed in order by the perfect fifth and the major triad (in a minor context, the minor triad is only slightly more dissonant than the major triad). The diatonic set, with its many fifths and only two minor seconds, is the most consonant seven-note collection. The most dissonant level is the chromatic collection. The space maximizes consonance and orders it hierarchically.

Any chord in any key can be represented by a configuration of the basic space. Figure 2.12b shows $V^7/\mathbf{d}$. A distance algorithm transforms one configuration into another and measures the distance traversed, employing three factors that combine additively: the number of moves on the chromatic cycle of fifths to reach another key, for instance C major to G major; the number of moves on the diatonic cycle of fifths to reach another chord within a key, for instance the tonic of C major to the dominant of C major; and the number of new pitch classes in the new configuration, weighted according to psychoacoustic salience as represented in the basic space. The algorithm gives as output the number of distance units from one chord to another. For example, the distance from I/$\mathbf{C}$ to V/$\mathbf{C}$ is 5; from I/$\mathbf{C}$ to I/$\mathbf{G}$ it is 7; from I/$\mathbf{C}$ to $V^7/\mathbf{d}$ it is 9.

Distances among chords and keys can be mapped geometrically so that distances in the space correspond to distances computed by the distance algorithm. Figure 2.13 gives an approximate mapping called chordal-regional space. The boldface letters represent the tonic of each key, and surrounding each tonic are the other chords within its key orbit. Within each key, fifth-relations appear on the vertical axis and diatonic third-relations on the horizontal axis. The keys are likewise arranged with fifth-relations on the vertical axis and third-relations on the horizontal axis alternating with parallel major-minor keys. At both the chord and key levels, chordal-regional space can be extended and wrapped around on both axes to form two orthogonal cylinders or a four-dimensional sphere. It resonates with several spaces in the history of music theory, notably those of Weber (1821–24) and Schoenberg

III	V	vii°	iii	V	vii°	III	V	vii°	iii	V	vii°
VI	**e**	III	vi	**G**	iii	VI	**g**	III	vi	**B♭**	iii
ii°	iv	VI	ii	IV	vi	ii°	iv	VI	ii	IV	vi

III	V	vii°	iii	V	vii°	III	V	vii°	iii	V	vii°
VI	**a**	III	vi	**C**	iii	VI	**c**	III	vi	**E♭**	iii
ii°	iv	VI	ii	IV	vi	ii°	iv	VI	ii	IV	vi

III	V	vii°	iii	V	vii°	III	V	vii°	iii	V	vii°
VI	**d**	III	vi	**F**	iii	VI	**f**	III	vi	**A♭**	iii
ii°	iv	VI	ii	IV	vi	ii°	iv	VI	ii	IV	vi

Figure 2.13. A portion of chordal-regional space.

([1954] 1969), and it has an interesting noncongruent relationship to Riemann's (1882, 1915) *Tonnetz*.[12] It is illuminating to trace the progression of events in a piece as a path through chordal-regional space. Hearing a tonal piece is like taking a pitch-space journey.

Just as there are many possible routes between cities, so there are many routes from one chord in one key to another chord in the same or another key. A core assumption in TPS is the principle of the shortest path; that is, listeners understand a progression in the most efficient way. For example, given a C major tonic chord, a G major chord is most likely heard as the dominant of C major, not, for instance, as the subdominant of D major or the mediant of E minor. Tonic orientation is established by the same principle: given the available pitches and chords in a time span, the tonic is found by the shortest path. The first pitch or first triad at the beginning of a piece sounds like a tonic because the shortest distance is from an event to itself, but other evidence may

12. For discussion, see Cohn 2011; Lerdahl 2015a. Unlike TPS's model of pitch space, tonal spaces in the *Tonnetz* tradition, such as Cohn (2012), are flat rather than hierarchical. They are based only on triads as pitch-class triangles and their transformations. Consequently, they are unable to represent nonharmonic tones, seventh chords, chord roots, scales, or keys. The lack of hierarchy also leads *Tonnetz* models to the dubious result that triads related by thirds are more proximate than are triads on the cycle of fifths.

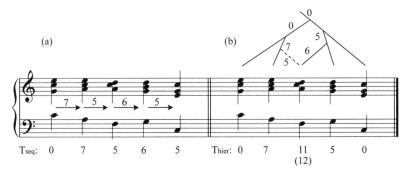

Figure 2.14. Two ways of calculating tension. T$_{seq}$ = sequential tension; T$_{hier}$ = hierarchical tension.

intrude to cause a reinterpretation. Think, for example, of the beginning of Beethoven's Ninth Symphony.

With the basic space and its distance metrics at hand, TPS quantified the increase or decrease in tension between two events by the distance between them. It proposed two ways to calculate distance tension, reflecting two ways of hearing music. The simpler hypothesis, illustrated in figure 2.14a, is that listeners hear music sequentially from one event to the next, without memory of previous events or expectation of events to come. As the numbers in figure 2.14a suggest, the rise and fall of tension in a sequential analysis tends to be quite flat. The second hypothesis, illustrated in figure 2.14b, is that listeners hear events hierarchically, an act that depends on both memory (right branching) and expectation (left branching). Distance is calculated additively down the branches of a prolongational tree. Figure 2.14b shows an increase in tension to the middle of the progression, followed by a relaxation into the cadence. The zero distance between the first and last events means that they are the same chord; that is, the progression as a whole prolongs a C major triad.

TPS (143) speculated that naive listeners tend toward sequential hearing and experienced listeners toward hierarchical hearing. After TPS's publication, Krumhansl and I undertook an extensive empirical study of the theory's predictions of tonal tension in music from Bach to Messiaen (Lerdahl and Krumhansl 2007). The study provided strong evidence that listeners, regardless of musical training, hear tension not sequentially but hierarchically.

Some scholars have downplayed the psychological relevance of event hierarchies in favor of statistical learning (Huron 2006), schematic patterns (Gjerdingen 2007), or nonhierarchical mathematical modeling (Tymoczko 2011). From these perspectives, the positing of hierarchical structures may seem unnecessary, a figment of the theoretical imagination. Krumhansl's and my study challenges such views by giving evidence of nonlocal, long-range dependencies in musical sequences. The issue of nonlocal dependencies is worth emphasizing because statistical methods or local formalisms such as Markov processes lack the capacity to represent them.[13]

In addition to tension calculated by hierarchical distance, the tension model includes two other aspects of tension: surface (or sensory) dissonance and tonal attraction. A purely psychoacoustic treatment of surface dissonance (such as Hutchinson and Knopoff 1978) would be inappropriate for a tonal idiom such as Schubert's. Listeners hear common-practice music through the filter of its well-developed syntax in which dissonance plays a categorical role. What matters most about dissonance in the Classical idiom is not instrumental timbre, register, or chord spacing, which are variable factors in any psychoacoustic measure, but whether a pitch is harmonic or nonharmonic according to the syntax, what inversion a chord is in, and what the melodic tone above a chord is. The dissonance component specifies a weighted tally of these features, with nonharmonic tones the most weighted since they generally involve dissonant intervals.

---

13. Koelsch and colleagues (2013) also provides evidence of the perception of hierarchical structure by manipulating global prolongational connections in paired phrases of two Bach chorales. While more limited in scope than Krumhansl's and my study (2007), their work takes the important step of providing evidence at a neuroscientific level.

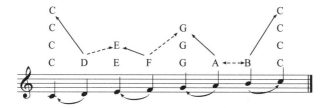

Figure 2.15. Strong stepwise attractions of diatonic scale degrees in the context of I/**C**.

The attraction component addresses the subjectively felt urge of pitches and chords to move strongly or weakly to other pitches and chords. For example, the leading tone strongly seeks the tonic pitch, and V^7 wants to resolve on I. These tendencies are asymmetric: the tonic pitch does not strongly seek the leading tone, nor does I seek V^7. Bharucha (1984a) offers a psychological account of this phenomenon for melody, based on factors of pitch proximity and relative stability: an unstable pitch anchors on a subsequent pitch that is nearby and more stable. TPS generalizes and quantifies these factors to develop a quasi-force-field in which all pitches and chords move. As with distance tension and surface dissonance, the attraction component gives a single output number for the attraction between two pitches or chords. A strong attraction causes a tension that is complementary to the tension created by pitch-space distance.

The factors of relative proximity and stability elucidate familiar intuitions about scale degrees. The solid arrows in figure 2.15 show the strongest stepwise attractions in pitches of the C major scale. The strongest is from B to C, since B is a half step from C and the differential of instability to stability is greatest from B to C. Next is from F to E, again because of the half-step motion. Third is the attraction of D to C, then A to G. In both, the instability-to-stability factor is strong, but the proximity factor is weaker because the anchor is a whole step instead of a half step away. The dashed arrows show secondary attractions, F to G and D to E, and finally the comparatively weak mutual attraction of A and B. Not shown are nonstepwise attractions among members of a triad, weak attractions of stable to unstable pitches, or very weak attractions between distant pitches. In short, a scale degree is not a conceptual primitive but a structure made up of a location in the basic space and consequent attractive forces exerted on it.[14]

A strong attraction induces an expectation that the attractor will occur next. In the Schubert, the E♮ in bar 12, supported by V/vi, implies that F will follow. As in Meyer (1956, 1973) and Narmour (1990), expectations can be realized or denied, and an unexpected realization, such as E♭ instead of F in bar 13, can be experienced as a surprise.

Figure 2.16 shows an approximated tension curve for the first period of the *Moment Musical,* based on combined calculations from hierarchical distance tension, surface dissonance, and melodic attraction. Both phrases show an overall increase and then decrease in tension. In the first phrase, tension is highest in the approach to I/V in bars 6–7. In the second phrase, a somewhat higher state of tension is reached in the approach to V/vi in bars 10–11.

Distant modulations yield higher tension than do nearby modulations. Figure 2.17 represents the *Moment Musical*'s modulations by distance units in chordal-regional space. The distances from the global tonic to its tonicized dominant and to the dominant of its relative minor are comparatively small. In the middle section, the tonic of the flat submediant, F♭ (notated by Schubert in E major), is reached via the intermediate stage of the parallel minor. The reprise takes the modula-

---

14. The theoretical literature abounds in approaches to diatonic scale degrees and their melodic tendencies. Here are a few instances since 1950. Zuckerkandl's (1956) account leads him to assert a nonphysical plane of existence with its own (unspecified) laws. Huron (2006) observes that scale-degree tendencies reflect the statistics of melodic occurrence in a large corpus of folk melodies and argues that no explanation beyond exposure is necessary. This account is insufficient. Of course exposure influences learning, but supporting the statistical patterns are the structure of pitch space and the psychoacoustic and cognitive factors that underlie it. Rings (2011) appeals to the philosophical notion of qualia—the ineffable subjective experience of redness or wetness, for instance—to account for intuitions about scale degrees. This appeal does not explain anything. In an approach that influenced my own thinking, Larson (2004, 2012) invokes the metaphorical forces of magnetism, gravitation, and inertia, based

Figure 2.16. Approximated tension curve for the first period of the *Moment Musical*.

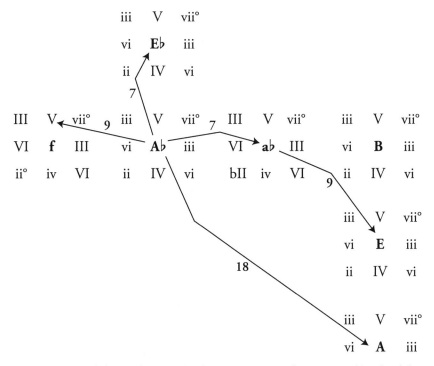

Figure 2.17. Modulation distances in the *Moment Musical,* represented in chordal-regional space.

tion one step further to the flat supertonic **B**♭♭ (A major): I/A♭→I/♭**II**. This moment is disruptive not only because of the dissonant inverted dominant seventh in bars 65–67 but also because the modulation is direct, only hinting beforehand at the intermediate stage of the parallel minor (bars 61–65). In addition, since tension is inherited down the prolongational tree, subordinate events in foreign keys receive still higher tension numbers than do their local tonics.

---

on Arnheim's (1954) ideas about forces in a visual field. Larson critiques TPS's attraction component. Indeed, Lerdahl and Krumhansl (2007) found that TPS's melodic attraction algorithm is empirically less accurate than its chord-distance and surface-distance algorithms. I have revised the attraction algorithm accordingly but await further testing before submitting it for publication.

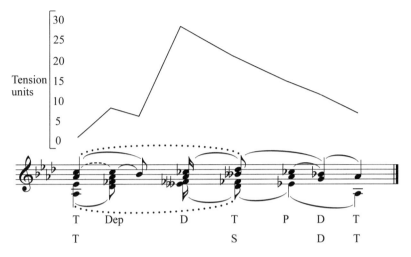

Figure 2.18. Prolongational structure, function analysis, and tension curve for the final phrase of the *Moment Musical* (repetitions omitted).

Figure 2.18 gives the prolongational structure, function analysis, and tension curve for the final phrase of the *Moment Musical*. For convenience, repetitions within the phrase are omitted. The dotted slurs show the tension toward I/♭**II**, after which there is a gradual relaxation to the final cadence in the (implied) parallel minor. The high point of tension of the phrase, indeed of the entire piece, is the dissonant V7/♭**II** in bars 65–67. This disruptive moment illustrates a fundamental feature of tonal music, the dialectic between salience and stability. Often an event or passage that is highly prominent is also highly unstable, tense, and subordinate in the prolongational hierarchy.

A full analysis of the *Moment Musical* would show an overall tension curve with increasingly climactic waves of tension and relaxation. The high tension arcs surrounding the arrivals in A♭ minor, E major, and A major relate to Cone's (1982) discussion of the piece's "promissory note": E (bar 12) prepares the augmented 6th on F♭ (bars 17 and 25), which in turn sets up the modulation to ♭**VI** (bars 36–39); similarly, the augmented 6th on F♭ (bar 41) suggests its enharmonic reinterpretation as

V⁷/♭II, which passes through I/♭II (bars 68 and 73). This pitch-class/harmonic development is implicative rather than hierarchical and hence lies outside of the scope of the GTTM/TPS theory as it stands. But the theory's hierarchical components, most tangibly those that analyze tonal tension, underlie and inform this logic. It is also worth noting in this connection that the extended consequent phrase (bars 61–77) that includes the A major passage is unstable in its grouping and metrical structures, just as was the E major passage discussed earlier. Pitch and rhythm work together to intensify waves of tension.

TPS and Lerdahl and Krumhansl (2007) devote so much effort to developing and testing the tension model because it has long been my conviction that patterns of tension and relaxation lie at the heart of musical understanding and expression. The three subcomponents of the model give an account that is multidimensional and fine-grained. The 2007 study demonstrated that intuitions of tension are robust, using different experimental procedures and with little discrepancy among listeners or across musical styles. The notion of tonal tension is more than a metaphor. It is an essential part of the musical experience.

The flowchart in figure 2.19 summarizes the theoretical topics covered by the analysis of the *Moment Musical*. The rhythmic components of grouping and meter (figures 2.5–6) together help form the time-span segmentation and time-span reduction (figure 2.7). The interaction principle (figure 2.8) controls levels of time-span reduction as input to the corresponding prolongational reduction (figure 2.9). Harmonic function is an outcome of prolongational position (figure 2.9). The pitch-space component replaces GTTM's underspecified stability conditions. Its distances are calculated algebraically but can be represented geometrically (figures 2.12–13). The model enables the quantification of sequential and hierarchical tension-relaxation patterns based on perceived distance (figure 2.14). Distances are calculated by the principle of the shortest path, a principle that also establishes tonic orientation at various levels of organization. Distances down the prolongational tree measure a primary aspect of tonal tension. A second aspect of tension

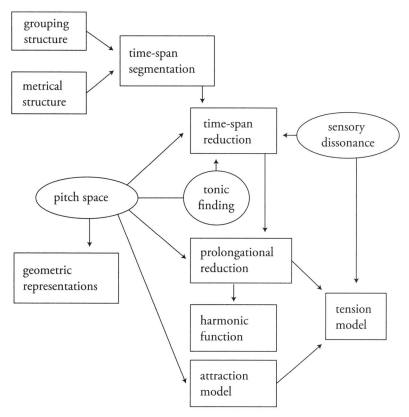

Figure 2.19. Flowchart of the components of the combined GTTM/TPS theory.

comes from surface dissonance. A third aspect results from the attraction of pitches and chords to one another and the resulting expectations thereby engendered (figure 2.15). All of these components culminate in the tension model, which produces a composite tension curve for a musical passage or piece (figure 2.16).[15]

15. The version of this graph in Lerdahl (2009) includes a component called prolongational good form, which regulates branching patterns (see Lerdahl 2001b, 25–29). I do not include it here because this chapter has not engaged with it. Besides, the principle of the shortest path usually suffices for assigning coherent patterns of tension and relaxation without any need to invoke prolongational good form.

The number of components in the flowchart reflects the scope of a theory that unites rhythmic hierarchies, pitch-event hierarchies, and the tonal hierarchy within an overarching framework. The components and their connections are all motivated theoretically and psychologically, and the empirical evidence justifies them.[16] Indeed, there are other aspects of music that the theory does not address thoroughly, above all associative structures—in particular, the omnipresent factor of parallelism between passages and implicative features of motivic and harmonic development. If these aspects were properly theorized, the flowchart would be even more complex.

The behavioral sciences have oscillated historically between, on the one hand, minimal assumptions of cognitive structure in favor of stimulus conditioning or statistical learning and, on the other, maximal hypotheses of rich cognitive structure, whether innate or learned. The former tendency is motivated by a drive for parsimony, the latter by a search for explanatory adequacy. The GTTM/TPS project takes a maximal perspective.

16. For example, Deliège (1987) and Frankland and Cohen (2004) on local grouping rules; Palmer and Krumhansl (1990) and Large and Palmer (2002) on meter; Palmer and Krumhansl (1987) on time-span reduction; Dibben (1994) and Bigand and Pineau (1997) on prolongational hierarchies and expectancy; Bigand, Parncutt, and Lerdahl (1996), Krumhansl (1996), Smith and Cuddy (2003), and Lerdahl and Krumhansl (2007) on pitch space and tonal tension.

CHAPTER THREE

On the Musical Capacity

This chapter addresses the nature and limitations of the musical mind, based on a variety of ideas and evidence. I shall traverse only a portion of this vast terrain but nevertheless hope to cover enough of it to convey a coherent picture.

If language were the topic, one would speak of the language capacity in terms of linguistic universals or universal grammar (Chomsky 1965). In talking with musicians, however, I have found that the term *universal* often raises red flags and causes misunderstanding. So I shall avoid it and refer instead to the musical capacity or the musical mind. Indeed, *universal* is a confusing word because it glosses over the distinction between cultural and psychological universals. A cultural universal in music is a feature that belongs to music in all cultures. To such a notion one can always find an exception. A psychological universal, in contrast, is a structural resource or propensity of the musical mind. This is my subject.

The study of any perceptual domain must specify what the basic objects of analysis are. For GTTM, as in much music theory, the basic object is the pitch event—that is, a pitch or chord occurring at a given point in time. This unit can be generalized to include nonpitch events. From the perspective of psychoacoustics or computer music, however, one might choose a more fine-grained level for the object of analysis, such as the attack-sustain-decay of a pitch or details in its spectral makeup. From a spectromorphological perspective (Smalley 1997; Thoresen 2007), one might instead focus on the sound shapes of pitches, timbres, and rhythms considered as unified gestures. Here I shall follow GTTM's conception of "event" while recognizing that it is also valid to study sub- or superobjects, depending on circumstances.

Albert Bregman's (1990) research on auditory scenes bears on the question of the musical object of analysis. The auditory system registers acoustic signals from multiple simultaneous sources and parses them into identifiable streams of sound. At this moment, at my desk, I hear two streams, clicking from my typing and chirping of birds outside the window. Within each stream, clicks and chirps have internal acoustic structure, but the perception is of clicks and chirps per se. These are events in GTTM's sense. Bregman's work exhaustively explores the many variables under which sounds fuse into single auditory objects or segregate into streams of objects.

How many objects can the auditory system process simultaneously? Cognitive scientists have determined that humans have three intuitive ways of dealing with number quantities: (1) by the natural number system; (2) by accurate estimate of large quantities; (3) by automatic and exact recognition of up to three or possibly four objects (Dehaene 1997). The number system needs little comment here. If you are asked what the number is after 98, you know it is 99. People are very good at estimates of large quantities; for example, if there are two piles of 100 blue and yellow marbles, they know at a glance that the pile with 75 blue and 25 yellow marbles has more blue marbles than the pile with 60 blue and 40 yellow marbles. The third category, automatic and precise recognition of small numbers, pertains to the processing question. If there are three marbles on a table, you see three immediately; you don't have to count. But if there are more than four marbles, immediate recognition fails and you must chunk them into smaller groupings. It turns out that infants and many higher mammals also possess the ability to estimate large quantities and automatically recognize very small numbers. These are phylogenetically ancient ways of dealing with quantity, part of the core knowledge that humans inherit through evolution (Hauser and Spelke 2004; Carey 2009).

Several years ago I brainstormed with Marc Hauser, a cognitive scientist who specializes in animal cognition, about how small-number processing shows up in music. We came up with this list:

(1) It is virtually impossible to distinguish more than three contrapuntal lines at a time. A four-voice Bach fugue fuses harmonically.

(2) Three instruments playing simultaneously can be heard distinctly, but more instruments blend into perceptual unity.

(3) Weak beats appear not at four or five strong beats apart at the next smaller level but require an interposed metrical level that subdivides strong beats by two or three.

(4) Four or five motivic or phrasal groupings at a single grouping level do not fall under a larger group without further subdivision. In Beethoven's piano sonatas, for example, larger groupings always divide into two or three groups at the next smaller level.

The list encompasses diverse musical phenomena under one principle. More than three inputs of the same kind overload processing channels. This constraint is not about music per se. It is a general phenomenon that includes music.

Case (1) concerns streams or polyphonic lines (for related discussion, see Huron 2001). Case (2) is the timbral counterpart to (1). Bregman's principles are gestalt in nature, so it should not be surprising that some of them, in particular those of proximity and similarity, also appear in GTTM's local grouping rules. Streaming consists of groupings in horizontal instead of vertical slices. Cases (3) and (4) pertain not to musical objects but to structures inferred from them. GTTM states case (3) as an idiom-specific preference rule. Given the evidence about small-number processing, it seems that the rule is general. GTTM does not treat case (4) in its rule system; this was an oversight.

Taking a hint from case (3), let us consider in more detail the organization of and constraints on metrical organization. Meter is a mental construct, a looping pattern of strong and weak beats, which the listener infers from a musical surface if the stresses at the surface are sufficiently regular. Some kinds of music—the beginning of a raga, much shakuhachi music, Gregorian chant under certain performance assumptions, some kinds of recitative, a fair amount of contemporary art music—are not metrical; that is, when listening to these kinds of music, listeners do not infer a recurring pattern of strong and weak beats because the musical surface does not provide enough cues for periodicity. Meter is an option, not a requirement, for music. But most kinds of music induce some kind of metrical structure, indicating that metrical organization is a propensity of musical behavior. Meter measures time; it permits the precise temporal location of events. When you hear metrical music, you intuitively know where you are. When you hear nonmetrical music, the sense of time is vague; you feel that you are more or less, rather than exactly, at this or that point in time.

Metrical perception depends partly on speed (Clarke 1999; London 2012). The perception of beats blurs at very fast rates, such as a tenth of a second, and becomes increasingly inaccurate above 1.5 seconds. Accuracy peaks at about ⅔ or ¾ of a second. A rate around this peak is the perceptually most prominent metrical level, or tactus, the level at which dancers are most likely to step or conductors wave their arms. It is close to the heart rate. Recent work in neuroscience suggests neural oscillatory constraints as a biological link (Large and Snyder 2009; Doelling and Poeppel 2015). Once an optimal pulsation is inferred, other beat levels are measured in relation to it. Depending on the pattern of stresses, the listener may infer metrical levels larger than the tactus, permitting an expanded yet still accurate sense of temporal location.

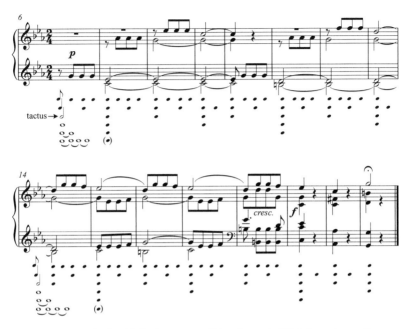

Figure 3.1. Metrical grid for bars 6–21 of Beethoven's Fifth Symphony, I.

The metrical grid for bars 6 to 21 of the first movement of Beethoven's Fifth Symphony, given in figure 3.1, illustrates this point. The music evokes five metrical levels, the largest of which covers four bars, or 2.5 seconds assuming a metronome marking of half note = 96. If heard in isolation, a rate of 2.5 seconds would not be perceived very accurately, but because of the grid it is heard and measured in terms of ½ and ¼ of that rate; and ¼ of 2.5 seconds equals 0.625 seconds, which lies within the optimal tactus range.[1]

1. Somewhat unusually, Beethoven notated the tactus at the measure level because other passages in the movement have irregular phrase lengths, and it was a notational convention of the time to avoid a change in time signature. The quarter-note level is realized not by attack points at the surface but by the overall grid pattern. Beethoven saves quarter notes for the second theme group. The Schubert *Moment Musical* discussed in chapter 2 likewise has the tactus at the measure level, again because of irregular phrase lengths. Until the phrasal and metrical irregularities of the middle section, one hears the piece in 6/4 rather than 3/4.

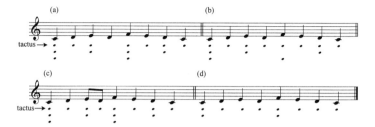

Figure 3.2. Ill-formed metrical grids: (a) an absent beat, (b) a nonhierarchical grid, (c) unequal beats, (d) strong beats more than three beats apart.

What are the abstract constraints on a metrical organization? Or, in GTTM's terms, what are the well-formedness conditions for a metrical grid? Figure 3.2 presents four ill-formed grids as counterexamples. In case (a), there is a gap in the smallest metrical level, so that a tactus-level event incorrectly does not receive a beat. The prohibition of a gap does not disallow extrametrical events such as grace notes or fermatas. In case (b), the F is assigned a large-level beat that is not a beat at the next smaller level. This is nonsensical, for meter is organized hierarchically. In case (c), beats at the tactus and next larger level are not equally spaced. The eighth notes require another, smaller metrical level. A condition of meter is that beats be equally spaced enough to be quantized as functionally isochronous. This condition does not prohibit gradual acceleration or retardation. In case (d), strong beats are four beats apart, with no metrical differentiation in between, thus violating the principle that strong beats be two or three beats apart. This principle not only meets the small-number criterion but also ensures that a weak beat is adjacent to at least one strong beat.

Well-formed metrical grids can be broadly classified as in figure 3.3: (a) multiple levels of beats, with equidistant beats at each level and beats two or three beats apart at the next larger level (as in Western tonal music); (b) multiple levels of beats, with equidistant beats at the smallest level, beats two or three beats apart within the next level, and often

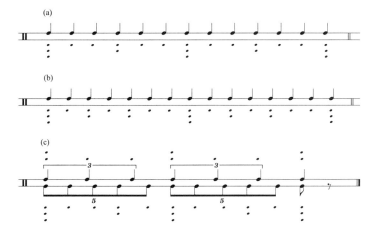

Figure 3.3. Three types of well-formed metrical grids: (a) equidistant beats at each level, (b) a combination of two and three beats apart within a given level, (c) multiple beat streams with in-phase larger beats.

equidistant beats at a still larger level (as in much Balkan music); (c) multiple beat streams, with often noncoincident beats at a smaller metrical level but equidistant, coincident beats at a larger level (as in certain virtuosic passages in North Indian music).

Each of the three grid types can combine in different ways within its own type—for instance, different combinations of two and three beats apart in type (a)—and each can combine with the other types. The result is a small combinatorial explosion of possible grids. A given musical style typically employs a small subset of possible grids.

Listeners infer particular metrical grids by finding the best match, or fewest violations, between stress patterns in the musical signal and the repertory of available grids in the style in question. This process happens automatically and quickly. (Turn on the radio to hear music and notice that it takes just a moment to find the beat.) GTTM explains through its metrical preference rules how the process happens. Some rules appear to be psychologically general, especially those that incorporate gestalt principles, while others are style specific. No doubt the list of factors is incomplete, if only because of the theory's orientation to Western tonal music. Comparative study of music from around the globe promises to enrich and correct hypotheses about the musical mind with respect not only to meter but also to other musical components.

Sometimes the metrical grid that an indigenous listener assigns to a rhythmic sequence seems counterintuitive to an outsider. Gerhard Kubik (2010, 106) reports that he had this experience with certain sub-Saharan African rhythms, especially in West Africa. Such discrepancies arise from differences in cultural learning. Figure 3.4a gives a widespread African rhythm that is irregular and metrically ambiguous; that is, it can receive several acceptable metrical solutions. Figure 3.4b, following the principle that a stress tends to fall on a note that is longer than the previous note, interprets the rhythm in a changing meter that aligns quarter notes on downbeats when they occur after eighth notes. This interpretation has no syncopations—where syncopation is defined as a stress on a weak beat—at the price of abandoning a uniform meter. Figure 3.4c opts for a regular meter of 3/2, thereby treating notes 4, 5, and 6 as syncopations. Figure 3.4d does the same but in 12/8 meter, treating notes 2, 4, and 5 as syncopations. It turns out that Africans typically take the last interpretation and move their bodies in relation to it (Agawu 2006).

This rhythm has two group-theoretic properties that will pivot the discussion from metrical grids to pitch space.[2] First, the rhythm yields a unique pattern starting at any point in the sequence. Figure 3.5a identifies rhythmic events by number. The original African rhythm appears in the first bar, rotates by one step in the second bar, and another step in the third. The pattern does not duplicate before the rotation is exhausted. Figure 3.5b presents a counterexample with a repetitive

2. These group-theoretic properties were introduced with respect to musical scales by a number of theorists, including Gamer 1967; Balzano 1980; Browne 1981; Clough and Douthett 1991; and Agmon 1996. Balzano (1982) casts them in terms of Gibsonian perceptual psychology (Gibson 1966).

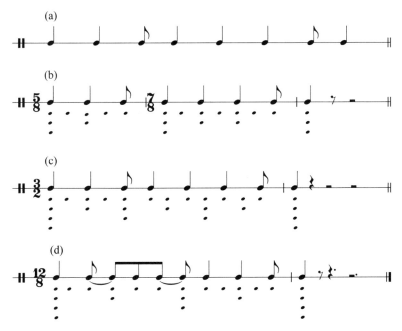

Figure 3.4. Metrical grids for a standard African rhythm: (a) the rhythm without metrical interpretation; (b) changing meter, following the stresses; (c) in 3/2 meter; (d) in 12/8 meter.

rhythmic pattern. By the third bar, the rotation already duplicates the first bar. This pattern is not unique.

Figure 3.6 illustrates the property of uniqueness in geometric format. Imagine that you are in a hexagonal room with equal sides and angles and no other distinguishing features. The vista is the same from every corner, as in figure 3.6a. But if the room has unequal sides distributed unevenly, as in figure 3.6b, the vista from each corner is distinct. In the same way, a rhythmic pattern exhibiting uniqueness provides more information about position than a nonunique pattern does. The musical mind is attuned to this property.

The second abstract property of the African rhythm is that its elements are distributed in a maximally even way, granted the asymmetry that necessarily results from five quarter and two eighth notes. Figures 3.7a–b

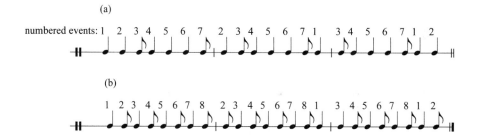

Figure 3.5. Rhythmic uniqueness and nonuniqueness: (a) rotation of the African rhythm, resulting in a different pattern each time; (b) rotation of a regular rhythm, resulting in duplication at the third rotation.

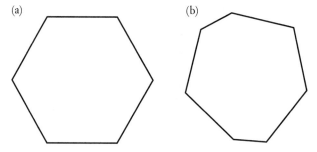

Figure 3.6. Uniqueness illustrated with polygons: (q) equilateral hexagon, (b) heptagon with two short and five long sides.

illustrate negatively by uneven distributions, in case (a) by two eighth notes bunched together at the beginning of the sequence, in case (b) with the eighths spread out only a little. In case (c), the eighths are distributed as evenly as possible, separated by two and then three quarter notes. This is a rotated version of the original African rhythm.

The psychological utility of the principle of maximal evenness is less apparent in the rhythmic than in the pitch domain. The African rhythm is isomorphic to the diatonic scale (Pressing 1983; Rahn 1983), which like the rhythm is made up of two elements, one twice the size of

Figure 3.7. Rhythmic maximal evenness, illustrated with durations from the African rhythm: (a–b) uneven distributions, (c) maximally even distribution.

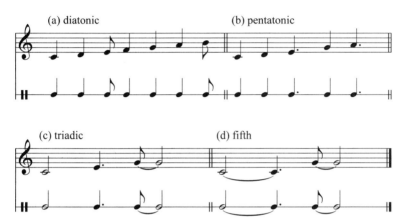

Figure 3.8. Mapping of the African and related rhythms onto pitch.

the other. Figure 3.8a shows that just as the rhythm has the step-duration pattern of quarter-quarter-eighth-quarter-quarter-quarter-eighth, so the major scale has the step-interval pattern of whole-whole-half-whole-whole-whole-half. This step-interval pattern is maximally even, given two step-sizes and seven pitches per octave. A related African rhythm in figure 3.8b also exhibits the properties of uniqueness and maximal evenness and is isomorphic to the pentatonic scale. Figures 3.8c and d extend the mapping further to the triad and perfect fifth, both of which again display uniqueness and maximal evenness if built from the elements of the diatonic or pentatonic scale. A maximally even scale minimizes confusions about steps and skips. In the diatonic scale, the interval of a second, whether major or minor, is always smaller than a third, which is always smaller than a fourth. This property does not obtain in other familiar scales such as the harmonic minor scale and the acoustic (ascending melodic minor) scale.

Balzano (1982) argues that the cultural pervasiveness of the diatonic and pentatonic scales is a consequence not of their familiar acoustic derivation via just intonation or the cycle of fifths but of the properties of uniqueness and maximal evenness within the 12-fold equal division of the octave. This argument is anachronistic, for these scales existed long before the invention of the equal-tempered chromatic scale. It is more plausible to claim a convergence between these properties and psychoacoustic consonance. The 12-fold division of the octave approximates the intervals derived by just intonation or Pythagorean tuning. Of the many possible equal divisions of the octave, only this division satisfies both psychoacoustic consonance and the two abstract properties.

Assuming the equal-tempered chromatic scale, the numbers 5 and 7 are not whole-number divisors of 12, so five- and seven-note scales divide the chromatic scale asymmetrically. Diatonic Western music cultivates even meters but asymmetrical pitch structures. Highly chromatic tonal music, however, frequently forsakes the property of uniqueness to explore full maximal evenness via whole-number divisors of 12. The divisors 3, 4, and 6 create the completely symmetrical augmented triad, diminished seventh chord, and whole tone scale, shown in figure 3.9a–c, respectively. Figures 3.9d–e fill in gaps in the augmented triad and diminished seventh chord, respectively, to yield the mostly symmetrical hexatonic and octatonic scales.

Chapter 2 discussed how in the diatonic system the cognitive distances among pitches, chords, and keys project geometrically into multidimensional structures. The asymmetrical diatonic scale transposes 12 times, and the major-minor system doubles this amount in diatonic basic space. These features lead to the complex geometry partially represented in figure 2.13 and enable the complex modulations that are characteristic of Schubert's music (among others). Equal-interval divisions of the octave, by contrast, give rise to nonunique scales and

Figure 3.9. Symmetrical divisions of the octave and related scales: (a) divisor 3 and the augmented triad, (b) divisor 4 and the diminished-seventh chord, (c) divisor 6 and the whole-tone scale, (d) the hexatonic scale fills in the augmented triad, (e) the octatonic scale fills in the diminished-seventh chord.

geometries that are comparatively simple and closed. The symmetrical hexatonic scale transposes only four times, the octatonic scale three times, and the whole-tone scale twice, leading to progressively smaller spaces. (For details, see Lerdahl 2001b, chapter 6.) Composers who have employed these scales and spaces feel their limits intuitively and typically leaven them by moving into diatonic space and back. Think, for example, of Debussy's piano prelude "Voiles" or the first movement of Stravinsky's *Symphony of Psalms.* Motion from one space to another may be termed hypermodulation, in contradistinction to standard modulation within a space. To achieve structural richness in its pitch organization, an idiom must have at its disposal multiple pitch-space dimensions, either within a space or across multiple spaces. Otherwise the possibilities are too narrow.[3]

It is useful to sort early twentieth-century composers between those who employed multiple tonal spaces and hypermodulation, such as Debussy, Scriabin, Stravinsky, and Bartók, and those who abandoned hierarchical pitch spaces in favor of great harmonic variety at the musical surface, such as Schoenberg and Webern in their atonal phases.

3. Messiaen (1944) speaks of the "charm of impossibilities" in connection with his modes of limited transposition, which include the whole-tone and octatonic scales. Where for him there is charm, for me there is limitation.

(a)   (b)

```
C                      C
C           G          C               •                        •
C     E     G          C               •          •             •
C  D  EF    G     A    BC               •     •    •      •      •
C C♯ D D♯ E F F♯ G G♯ A B♭ B C          • • • • • • • • • • • •
```

Figure 3.10. Formal similarity between pitch space and metrical grid: (a) I/**C** in diatonic space, (b) 12/8 metrical grid.

Schoenberg was well aware of tonal spaces, however, and tried to reestablish their equivalents in his 12-tone period (Schoenberg [1911] 1978; [1950] 1975, 214–44; [1954] 1969).

A revisit to the construct of the basic space will extend the comparison between rhythms and scales. Figure 3.10a repeats from figure 2.12a the basic space for a C major chord in C major, and figure 3.10b shows a grid for 12/8 meter. Evenness and unevenness aside, they look alike. Each structure forms a string of equidistant objects at the bottom level that loop in a repeating pattern, from octave to octave in pitch space and from measure to measure in metrical structure. If an object in either domain is stable or strong at one level, it is also an object at the next larger level. The formats are the same.

Just as metrical perception weakens at too fast or too slow a tempo, so pitch perception fades at registral extremes. Clarity of pitch perception peaks in a middle range a little above middle C (Terhardt, Stoll, and Seewann 1982). As with intervals between beats, pitch intervals are perceived categorically rather than absolutely (Burns and Ward 1984). It is difficult to distinguish extremely small interval differences in either domain. Yet scalar intervals are not very large, since otherwise there would be a scarcity of pitches per octave. The most frequent melodic intervals cross-culturally are small (Huron 2001). At least since Rousseau (1763), theorists have surmised that musical melody and the melody of speech are related, and the rise and fall of speech intonation usually covers small ranges from syllable to syllable. A major second, or an interval close to it, both permits a reasonable number of pitches per octave and facilitates the melodic approximation of speech contour. The melodic equivalent of the tactus is the major second.

Incidentally, grouping structure also has an equivalent of the tactus: the phrase. Subphrase groupings and multiple-phrase groupings are generally less salient, and often more ambiguous perceptually, than the phrase itself. Rothstein (1989) describes the phrase as the smallest grouping unit that projects significant tonal motion. In GTTM, a phrase is the smallest grouping unit that manifests tension and then relaxation into a cadence.

As with metrical grids, there are optional preferential constraints on the shape of basic spaces. We have encountered three of these in features of scales: uniqueness, maximal evenness, and optimal step sizes. A fourth constraint is that there be only two sizes of steps. A fifth constraint that applies not to rhythm but only to scales is that adjacent intervals within a level of a basic space be increasingly consonant from one level to the next higher level, as in diatonic/triadic basic space. To take a contrary example, one could imagine a basic space constructed so that the highest, modular level is not the octave but the major seventh, with the next lower level composed of major and minor thirds. Such an organization would not be supported by the relative sensory consonance of its intervals. The schema of a basic space is bound up with the perception of consonance and dissonance.

It is important in this connection to distinguish between sensory and musical consonance and dissonance. The consonance constraint refers to sensory dissonance, which is a product of the interaction of the acoustic signal with the auditory system and is not culturally or historically variable except on an evolutionary scale. Musical consonance and dissonance, in contrast, is a result of a given musical idiom and varies within limits from culture to culture. Intervals in Western tonality from the fifteenth through the nineteenth century act syntactically as either consonant or dissonant, whereas from a sensory perspective the transition from consonance to dissonance is gradual. When comparing

(a)   (b)

```
C
C               F♯                          C
C       E   F♯          B♭                  C                    G
C C♯  D♯ E   F♯ G    A B♭                   C D♭     E F   G A♭       B
C C♯ D D♯ E F F♯ G G♯ A B♭ B                C D♭ D E♭ E F F♯ G A♭ A B♭ B
```

Figure 3.11. Nondiatonic spaces, both oriented to C as tonic: (a) octatonic/
French-sixth space, (b) raag Bhairav.

intervals that are close in sensory consonance, syntactic treatments
may vary. In medieval music, a perfect fourth is more consonant than a
major or minor third, but in Classical tonality thirds are consonant and
the perfect fourth is dissonant in relation to the bass. In no culture,
however, is the octave treated as more dissonant than the major seventh. Sensory dissonance constrains variability in musical dissonance.

When the consonance constraint combines with the other constraints, we arrive at a sort of topography of basic spaces. For example,
the octatonic/French-sixth space in figure 3.11a—that is, a space of
French-sixth chords (the [0 2 6 8] tetrachord) built over an octatonic
collection, a structure central to Scriabin's late music—retains the
major and minor seconds of diatonic scale steps, but it drops uniqueness
and optimizes maximal evenness. In figure 3.11b, by contrast, the Indian
raag Bhairav flattens the second and sixth diatonic scale degrees,
thereby preserving uniqueness and abandoning evenness. (The chord
level is suppressed, in keeping with Indian practice.) The spaces in figure 3.11, though well formed, do not meet all the cognitively available
features of a basic space. That the diatonic and pentatonic spaces do
meet all of them may partly explain the prevalence of these scales historically and cross-culturally. The musical mind tends to exploit maximal structural possibilities.

A basic space and its attendant constraints are not an obligation but
a resource available to the musical mind. If an idiom employs a basic
space, the stabilities and instabilities thereby generated promote the
inference of complex event hierarchies; for, as outlined in chapter 2, the

distances computed from a basic space are a crucial input to prolongational reduction. The extent to which a basic space can support the emergence of an event hierarchy depends in part on how many of its constraints are operative. If an idiom does not employ a basic space, the inferred pitch structures will be limited in hierarchical depth, and structural richness may instead take place in another musical dimension. West African music is a good example of this: its relatively simple pitch organization is compensated by a complex rhythmic organization that depends in good part on its incorporation of uniqueness and maximal evenness in the rhythmic instead of pitch domain.

Pitches and chords in the context of a basic space create a force field of attractions, as discussed in chapter 2, so that an unstable pitch or chord metaphorically seeks resolution on a nearby stable pitch or chord. Following by analogy the abstract similarity between space and grid, TPS (288–97) proposes a theory of metrical attractions, so that a weak beat is strongly attracted to the following strong beat but not the reverse. This development lends dynamic treatment to rhythm as well as pitch. It also has consequences for performance. Just as a violinist may raise the leading tone, bringing it closer to the tonic and thereby increasing the need for resolution, so a conductor may delay an upbeat, as in a Viennese waltz, increasing its drive to land on the ensuing downbeat. Such deviations are part of what makes musical performance expressive.

The theory of attractions together with paths in pitch space has implications for intuitions about musical force and agency. The cognitive scientist Steven Pinker (1997) writes:

> Location in space is one of the two fundamental metaphors in language. The other is force, agency, and causation. Many cognitive scientists have concluded that a handful of concepts about places, paths, motions, agency, and causation underlie the literal or figurative meanings of tens of thousands of words and constructions in every language that has been studied. These concepts and relations appear to be the vocabulary and syntax of mentalese, the language of thought. (354–55)

Force translates into music if one imagines a melody traveling through tonal space. Like a spaceship traveling among the moons of Jupiter, the melody moves in a certain direction but is affected in its velocity and direction by the gravitational or attractive forces within the current tonal configuration. A nonchord tone may have little effect on its motion, but a nearby tonic has considerable mass and may bring the tonal spaceship to rest.

Pinker refers to a classic experiment by Heider and Simmel (1944) in which human subjects watch a cartoon film using three simple geometrical objects and a few lines.[4] As the objects move, the subjects interpret them as animate agents. Pinker (1997) writes:

> Agents are recognized by their ability to violate intuitive physics by starting, stopping, swerving, or speeding up without an external nudge. The agents are thought to have an internal and renewable source of energy which they use to propel themselves, usually in the service of a goal. (322)

Similarly, a melody or chord progression does not simply follow the inertial path of least resistance. It would quickly come to a stop unless enlivened by motion away from places that pull it toward rest. Such motion works against inertia as if caused by an animate agent. Furthermore, the motion causes an emotional response. Echoing Pinker, the neurologist Antonio Damasio (1999) writes:

> With a simple chip moving about on a computer screen, some jagged fast movements will appear "angry," harmonious but explosive jumps will look "joyous," recoiling motions will look "fearful." A video that depicts several geometric shapes moving about at different rates and holding varied relationships reliably elicits attributions of emotional state from normal adults and even children. (70)

Here is a central source of musical emotion. We internalize the motion of pitches and chords in reaction to tonal forces in musical space. We

---

4. Several versions of the Heider and Simmel cartoon experiment can be found online.

attribute agency and causation to musical motions that violate intuitive physics and inevitability to those that yield to musical momentum and force. The shape of the motions mirrors analogous trajectories in the physical world. We map particular musical gestures onto particular emotional qualities, again in reflection of real-world correspondences.[5]

Heider and Simmel's experimental subjects not only inferred agency and causation but also construed entire narratives from the motion of a few nonreferential triangles, circles, and lines. This result is suggestive for the study of musical narrative. As in their cartoon, pitches and rhythms need not take the course of least action but often move in manifold ways, some expected and some unexpected, as if by their own volition, forming connections, patterns, and oppositions—in short, behaving as if they are enacting a story. Moreover, a story is not just a sequence of events. It also has hierarchical structure in which some events are subordinate to others, creating patterns of tension and relaxation that are broadly analogous to the tension-relaxation patterns in prolongational reduction.

This discussion of metrical grids and pitch space—and, more briefly, of agency and narrative—gives rise to an overall picture in which the deepest features of the musical mind reside not at the stylistic surface of a given musical idiom but in the kinds of mental representation and organization that are available to the musical mind. This picture implies that exposure to statistical features of musical surfaces, while important in learning a musical idiom, is insufficient to account for musical understanding because the statistics alone provide little structure. In this connection, Krumhansl (1990) appeals not only to statistical distributions but also to cognitive reference points to explain her empirically derived tone profiles for which the basic space is a formal model. The idea comes from influential psychological research on categorization and prototypes (Rosch 1975; Rosch and Mervis 1975). Within

---

5. See Schlenker (2017) for related discussion in the context of a proposal for a theory of musical semantics.

a category there is typically an exemplar or reference point to which other members of the category relate. Krumhansl suggests that the tonic plays this role in tonality. The fifth and the third of a triad act as subsidiary reference points. These points correspond in my terms to relative tonal stability, and they function as points of tonal attraction.

Parncutt (1989) and Cariani (2001) attempt to ground the tone profile in psychoacoustics, Parncutt through Terhardt's (1974) virtual-pitch theory and Cariani through a periodicity-based computational model of pitch perception. It is indeed worth asking if psychoacoustics alone can explain the tone profile without invoking the cognitive schema of a basic space and its transformations. Parncutt has sought this outcome on grounds of theoretical parsimony, with qualified success. Cariani's model suggests that the cognitive schema arises from the converging harmonicity of temporally timed neural spikes. In my view, the schema is requisite for the cognitive system to function stably and efficiently.

Particular basic spaces are learned through exposure, but it seems that the format of a basic space and its metrical counterpart are not. Likewise, the human ability to form nested groupings of events and to relate events hierarchically, so that adjacency appears not only at the surface but also at underlying levels and sometimes at a considerable distance, would appear to belong to the musical capacity itself prior to the cultural exposure that shapes these structures in specific ways in particular cultures. Moreover, it is not only these kinds of structure that are available but also many of the principles by which they are implicitly constructed by the listener. (Here the discussion touches base with GTTM's provisional classification of its rules as either universal or idiom-specific [345–52]. No doubt the classification could be improved and enlarged by empirical and ethnomusicological research; see, for example, Clarke 2017.)

However, an argument for the prior availability of spaces, grids, groupings, and trees, along with many of the principles by which they are organized, does not entail a claim that they are Darwinian adaptations specifically for the musical capacity. Perhaps music itself, taken as a whole, is not adaptive. After all, unlike language, music does not appear to offer an evolutionary advantage. And so we arrive at the ultimate question about the musical capacity: what is the origin of music?

There have been two broad responses to this question. One is to offer reasons why music might be adaptive. Candidates include social bonding, joint action by synchronous behavior, mother-infant vocal interaction, and sexual selection (Wallin, Merker, and Brown 2001). Such speculations may have merit, but for the most part they are very general and difficult to substantiate. Since music leaves scarcely any fossils or ancient artifacts, confirmation of a particular claim for adaptation must be established not by physical evidence but indirectly by means of close structural analysis and through application of comparative methods from biology.[6]

The second response is to argue that music is not adaptive but a by-product of behaviors that are adaptive. That is, although music is shaped by evolution as a consequence of selective pressure on other capacities from which it draws, it is not itself a product of selective pressure. Pinker (1997, 534) asserts that music is "auditory cheesecake," by which he means that music tickles the brain's pleasure circuits. The pleasure responses for food and sex are adaptive, even if sometimes these instincts take a destructive turn. Music, he argues, piggybacks on pleasure.

Patel (2010) offers a more benign version of the nonadaptive position. Citing the plasticity of the brain in response to practice on an instrument or in therapeutic training after a brain lesion, he proposes that music enhances the brain in an individual's lifetime even if it is not adaptive on an evolutionary scale. He views the most distinctive aspects of music—pitch space and metrical structure—as derivative of other capacities: pitch space from a combination of cognitive reference points and statistical learning, metrical structure from vocal learning. As to the latter, our primate relatives do not entrain to a regular beat, much

6. See Honing (2018) for a current and wide-ranging survey of the origins of "musicality" (that is, of the musical capacity).

less to a multileveled metrical grid. Comparative studies of animal behavior suggest that only those animals that learn complex vocalizations, such as songbirds, are capable of such entrainment (Fitch 2006; Patel 2009). Apparently, metrical behavior is tied to brain regions implicated in motor control, and this is so even in distant species. There is a YouTube video of a cockatoo named Snowball dancing to rock music (Patel et al. 2009). A chimpanzee would never do that.

I prefer to approach the issue of the origin of music from another angle. I doubt the wisdom of treating music as if it were one thing. The boundaries of what constitutes music vary from culture to culture, historically and ethnographically. As reviewed in chapter 2, music has many parts, which is why the GTTM/TPS theory has many components. In my view, it is more fruitful to examine these components in detail than to begin with grand claims about Music.

Only after the individual components are reasonably well understood is it productive to ask which of them are special to music and which are shared with other capacities (Jackendoff and Lerdahl 2006). Briefly, grouping structure exists not just in music but is ubiquitous in human activity. The grouping capacity comes from general cognition. Streaming belongs to general auditory perception and visual perception. Meter has smaller scope: it appears to be shared only with poetry and dance. Contour and timbral patterning are shared with language. Recursive headed hierarchies belong not only to musical reductions but also to syntax and phonology in language and to complex actions such as making a cup of coffee (Jackendoff 2009). Nested patterns of tension and relaxation pertain not only to prolongational structures in music but also to a variety of temporal activities, physical and mental. Tonal attractions are a special case of the mental organization of objects or events around proximate reference points. In all these aspects, music shares with general phenomena.

The unique parts of music are in the pitch domain: fixed pitches and intervals, organized consonance and dissonance, harmony and counterpoint, the geometry of pitch space, tonal tension and attraction.

Some nonhuman species, such as songbirds and humpback whales, manifest fixed pitches and intervals but presumably not these other features. It is hard to imagine how these features could have adaptive value. They are products of culture.

Yet culture does not exist in a biological vacuum. There has been much interest lately in the origins of language, and this interest has spilled over to music because of the belief that the evolution of the two domains is intertwined (Brown 2000; Fitch 2010). Peretz and Coltheart (2003) report neuropsychological data on patients with brain lesions that point to common brain regions for rhythmic structures. Their research also suggests that pitch organization, on the one hand, and syntactic and semantic structures, on the other, belong to separate brain regions. Patel (2003, 2008) refines this view with the hypothesis that musical and linguistic syntaxes share brain-processing resources even though their representations in brain storage are separate. My own contribution to this area of research comes from a model of the sounds of poetry viewed as music (Lerdahl 2001a, 2013). The model is consistent with the empirical conclusions of Peretz and Patel and provides a formal framework for exploring these issues systematically.

The music-poetry model suggests that the component of linguistic theory that relates most strongly to music is not syntax with its parts of speech, nor semantics with its lexical entries and logical inferences, but phonology. This conclusion makes intuitive sense, for speech, like music, is organized sound in time. Rather than make this or that adaptive claim for music's origin, the model makes a detailed comparative analysis of the sound structure of music and language. Structures and principles common to both capacities can then be hypothesized as building blocks prior to their emergence. The building blocks are:

(a) hierarchically organized groupings of sound;
(b) stress patterns that, if sufficiently periodic, give rise to metrical grids;
(c) contour patterns;

(d) prolongational structures based on degrees of similarity among events in the time-span structure;

(e) similar or even identical principles by which these structures are generated;

(f) use of these structures for expressive purposes.

Darwin (1871) saw expressive animal vocalization as the source of the evolution of language and music. If you have a dog or cat or listen to birds, you will recognize that their vocalizations, whether about fear, food, sex, territory, or play, have the features of grouping, stress, intonation, recurrent timbral patterns, and, in the case of some animals such as songbirds, metrical structure. These are the common structures underlying the faculties of language and music. Their evolutionary history far precedes our primate ancestors. Animal vocalizations convey not only information but also strong emotional content, just as do speech and especially music. From this core, I argue, language grew in the direction of word meanings and their combinations, and music grew in the direction of fixed pitches and intervals and consequent complex pitch structures.

Musicians tend to have a bias about the specialness of music, claiming its extraordinary intellectual, emotional, and spiritual qualities as pristinely separate from the rest of human behavior. Yes, music is much more than a pleasure drug. Yet it is more satisfying to see many aspects of music as embodying fundamental features of our broader mental and emotional capacities, including its deep relationship to language. In this view, music steps off its pedestal to join the rest of human life.

CHAPTER FOUR

Cognitive Constraints Redux

At age eighteen, I composed a piece for mixed ensemble that opens with a 12-tone row in canon. I submitted the piece to a young composer competition and did not win. Shortly thereafter I read Stravinsky's first book of conversations with Robert Craft (Stravinsky and Craft 1959) and came across this remark:

> I did happen recently to look through a large number of student scores entered in a contest for a prize.... Mildly surprising was the discovery of so many scores aping the fashions of a decade ago. The series sticks out embarrassingly, usually in the first two bars, and after the series come the routine fugatos and canons. (109)

Was it my score that Stravinsky had glanced at? The possibility thrilled me even if he dismissed the music. But my lingering reaction was to ask why he objected to a clear presentation of the series at the beginning of a piece. After all, Mozart or Beethoven did not shy away from starting a piece on the tonic, and a jazz combo does not hesitate to open with the tune on which later improvisations take place. A few years later Milton Babbitt related to me how gleefully Stravinsky had told him that he would never find the 12-tone logic behind *Movements* for piano and orchestra.

One must understand the context of the aging Stravinsky's attitude. He was trying rather desperately to catch up with the younger generation, and he wanted to present a sophisticated front. In those days it was chic to appeal to a hidden order. In graduate school, my fellow students and I would pore over Boulez's *Le marteau sans maître,* which Stravinsky had declared to be a serial masterpiece, looking for the row and never finding it. A decade later, Lev Koblyakov (1977, 1993), an Israeli musicologist with the persistence of a Talmudic scholar, deciphered the serial organization of *Marteau* from obscure hints in Boulez (1971). Koblyakov later told me that he had tried to ascertain from Boulez directly if he had cracked the code. Boulez repeatedly put him off but finally gave in, took him to dinner, and laughingly acknowledged that he was right.

These anecdotes provide a backdrop for my reputedly infamous article "Cognitive Constraints on Compositional Systems" (hereafter CCCS) (Lerdahl 1988a), which begins with a short version of the story about *Marteau* and moves on to discuss the gap between composing method and heard result that is characteristic of so much modernist music. Before considering reactions to the article, let me review what it actually says.[1]

CCCS distinguishes between compositional and listening grammars. A compositional grammar is a conscious set of procedures employed by a composer to create a piece of music, diagrammed in figure 4.1a. The listening grammar in figure 4.1b takes a piece as input, rather than output, and models the listener's unconscious inference of its musical structure. Figure 4.1c combines figures 4.1a and 4.1b into one flowchart. Typically, a composer relies not only on the compositional grammar but also on unarticulated musical intuitions, yielding the added box in figure 4.1d. Now the piece of music has two inputs, the compositional grammar and intuitive constraints. The balance of the two depends on an individual composer's proclivities. The compositional grammar remains isolated, however, from the other compo-

---

1. CCCS develops a line of reasoning first set forth in GTTM, chapter 11. All of its arguments, including the issue of the cognitive opacity of 12-tone rows, are given deeper theoretical and historical context in TPS, chapters 7 and 8.

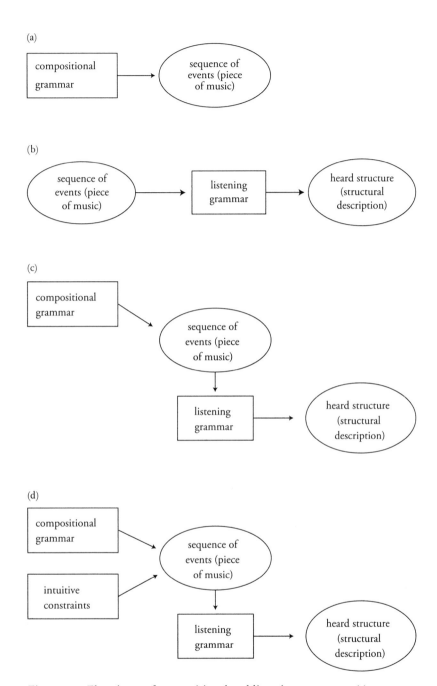

Figure 4.1. Flowcharts of compositional and listening grammars: (a) a
compositional grammar, (b) the listening grammar, (c) combination of
compositional and listening grammars, (d) addition of intuitive constraints,

(e)

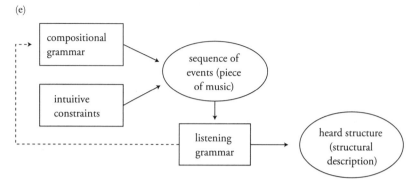

Figure 4.1 *(continued).* (e) the listening grammar as input to a compositional grammar.

nents. Consequently, it can be quite different from the listening grammar. To take a familiar example, Schoenberg composed with serial methods, but the sense that listeners make of his serial works is only indirectly related to their 12-tone organization.

CCCS then introduces a second distinction between natural and artificial compositional grammars. A natural compositional grammar emerges gradually in a culture, and its common usage ensures a connection with the listening grammar. An artificial grammar is the invention of an individual or small group. Artificial grammars appeared in Western art music in response to the decline of common-practice tonality and in the context of a modernist aesthetic that privileged innovation. The article accepts the prevalence of and need for artificial grammars in contemporary culture but urges that they be related to the listening grammar, as suggested by the dashed arrow in figure 4.1e. In this way the gap between method and result might be overcome.

The heart of CCCS consists of a list of cognitive constraints intended to give substance to the dashed arrow in figure 4.1e. The following constraints concern event hierarchies:

(1) discrete events,

(2) grouping,

(3) meter,

(4) pitch hierarchies.

The first constraint is fundamental: for syntax to have complexity, it must operate on discrete entities that combine in an indefinite number of ways. This is the principle of combinatoriality familiar in linguistics. A language without phonemes or words but merely gliding sounds would be so limited as to be useless. Likewise, musical syntax requires discrete sounds (usually pitches). The rest of the list comes from GTTM and was reviewed in chapter 2.

A second class of constraints addresses underlying materials:

(5) limits on interval size;

(6) pitch classes (octave generalization);

(7) psychoacoustic basis for stability conditions;

(8) equal temperament;

(9) uniqueness and maximal evenness;

(10) multidimensional pitch space;

(11) perceptual availability of levels of pitch space;

(12) a basic space to measure steps, skips, and melodic completion.

The constraints of interval size, octave generalization, and the psychoacoustic basis for stability conditions were dealt with in chapters 2 and 3, as were uniqueness, maximal evenness, and multidimensional pitch space. The equal-temperament constraint assists transposition at the price of sacrificing the fine intervallic distinctions and greater range of consonance and dissonance available from just intonation. The constraint on the availability of levels of pitch space concerns statistical learning: a highly nonredundant surface hinders the inference of a pitch-space schema. Finally, the article introduces, for the first time in my theoretical work, the construct of the basic space, a topic also discussed in chapters 2 and 3.

The next section of CCCS gives three reasons why 12-tone rows or serial structures are cognitively opaque:

(1) Serialism is a permutational system.

(2) Serialism attempts to neutralize sensory consonance and dissonance.

(3) Distances in 12-tone pitch space are perceptually problematic.

As mentioned in chapter 1, serialism is a permutational rather than elaborative system. Humans do not learn and remember permutations very well, especially so if the number of elements in a set exceeds three or four (as discussed in chapter 3). The second reason concerns the quixotic attempt to neutralize sensory consonance and dissonance under the banner of Schoenberg's "emancipation of dissonance," thereby removing a powerful tool for building hierarchical syntax (Schoenberg [1950] 1975, 216, 258–61). The third reason is the lack of a pitch space in which spatial distance correlates with psychophysical or cognitive distance. Pitch distance is first of all a factor of log-frequency distance, as in the distribution of pitches from low to high on a piano. Serial music, however, downplays such distances in favor of adjacencies in the row or other derived measures.

The cognitive opacity of 12-tone rows does not negate the validity of serial pieces. Indeed, Schoenberg denied in a letter to Rudolf Kolisch that recognition of a row was important in listening to 12-tone music (Schoenberg [1965] 1987, letter dated July 27, 1931). Instead, one hears a web of relationships emanating from the row. What the web of relationships amounts to cognitively has received comparatively little theoretical or empirical attention. It is striking that so simple an organization as the ordering of twelve objects and their elementary transformations (inversion, retrograde, retrograde inversion) are often difficult to perceive.

The final section of CCCS turns to aesthetic issues, beginning with the recognition that there is no obvious relationship between the comprehensibility of a piece and judgments of its artistic value. Nonetheless, wanting to put my cards on the table, I advance two general aesthetic claims:

(1) The best music uses the full potential of our cognitive resources.

(2) The best music arises from an alliance of the compositional and listening grammars.

The first claim finds a degree of specification in the second. That is, I advocate the adoption of some combination of the cognitive constraints under discussion.

In making these claims, CCCS does not attempt to define "the best music." That would be a hopeless quest, for aesthetic valuation is in good part culturally contingent and personally subjective. Moreover, aesthetic valuation depends on music's social function, and that too varies within and across cultures. The point, rather, is that beyond personal or cultural factors, intuitions of musical value rely on the ability of the musical mind to infer rich structure from a musical surface. The aesthetic claims favor music that promotes such inference.

To clarify the first claim, CCCS introduces a distinction between complexity and complicatedness. Musical complicatedness is a function of the number and variety of objects per unit of time. Musical complexity is a function of hierarchical depth. (The term *complexity* is used in many ways; this is my particular meaning for it.) I favor complexity and am neutral about complicatedness.[2]

The second aesthetic claim, the alliance of composing and listening grammars, repudiates the avant-garde attitude, or as I prefer to call it here, the progressive-modernist view that there are no limits to how music can develop.[3] Rather, there are infinite possibilities within limits

---

2. The notion of complicatedness relates to the mathematical concept of information. A greater number and variety of events per unit time yields both more information and a lower probability that any particular event will occur next. See Meyer 1967, 5–21; Temperley 2014.

3. The terms *avant-garde* and *modernist* can have divergent meanings. In particular, Bürger (1984) views modernism as emphasizing the autonomy of art and its internal historical development, in contrast to the avant-garde, which takes a critical, distancing, and often ironic or provocative stance in opposition to the commercialization of

imposed by human nature. The article closes with the assertion that the future of music lies less in progressive aesthetics than in the growing understanding of the musical mind.

I intended CCCS to be provocative. My hope was to influence how the contemporary-music world thinks about compositional method, the musical mind, and progress. But I was surprised by the extent of the hostile reception of the article in modernist musical circles. I was accused of trashing serial music, promoting retro-populist trends, and holding fascistic views of inherited abilities. Some responses were willful misconstructions of what I wrote, and on one occasion I responded in print (Lerdahl 1996). I do not want to rehash these instances. Yet it is instructive to reflect in a general way on why reactions were so antagonistic.

It is understandable that musical modernists would recoil in a stylistic sense at some of the prospects I set before them. Clear projection of grouping and meter, hierarchical event structures, pitch space with its representation of harmonic roots and levels of scales and chords—all of it smacks of traditional stylistic features that most modernists have rejected as outmoded. CCCS asserts that a rich mental representation of the structure of a composition involves some combination of these features.

The nub of the stylistic objection is tonality, in the broad sense of pitch centricity. Any hierarchical pitch organization entails centricity, independently of whether or not the music is diatonic or triadic. The central pitch or tonic dominates the prolongational tree as the reference point, the point of stability from which tension arises and to which it resolves. (Nota bene: I mean hierarchical pitch organization in the sense of the listening grammar, for a cognitively inaccessible composing grammar such as that for *Marteau* can also be described as hierarchical.) And a hierarchical pitch organization is strengthened when

---

art in a society dominated by modern capitalism. In his terms, the present discussion refers not to the avant-garde but to the strand of modernism that sees art as progressing dialectically along inevitable lines of development.

strong differences in sensory consonance and dissonance reinforce syntactic distinctions between stability and instability. This is as true of the music of Machaut or Messiaen as it is of Mozart.

Because the musical mind gravitates toward reference points, hence hierarchical pitch structures, an insistence on avoiding tonality, broadly conceived, is bound to be a passing phenomenon in the grand sweep of music history. The phenomenon will not pass quickly, however, for nothing is more conventional, hence more resistant to change, than musical modernism in its current institutionalized phase. In the late nineteenth and early twentieth centuries, modernism meant breaking of rules by individual artists in order to explore new territory. Now it means adherence to accepted aesthetic and stylistic precepts that crystallized over half a century ago. Musical modernism has largely been in stasis since then, in the sense of Meyer (1967), whose conception of stasis includes local variety within a global framework with little trajectory. Think of the radical changes in style every forty or fifty years from the seventeenth century to the mid-twentieth century. Since then the trajectory of overall change has stalled.

It must be admitted, however, that CCCS's emphasis on diatonic and triadic features was overdone. Indeed, with rare exception, it contradicted my own practice as a composer. The article had this emphasis because its ideas developed from GTTM, which was still new in 1988. The most insightful criticism came from the Belgian musicologist Célestin Deliège, who pointed out at a conference[4] that most music, historically and geographically, is less hierarchical than the music of the European Classical period that is GTTM's locus of study. He thought that CCCS overemphasized hierarchy and that other kinds of structure should be considered from a cognitive standpoint. Yet he agreed with the article's premise that the gap between compositional and listening grammars is a serious problem. I do not know what other

---

4. I first presented the material in CCCS at the conference "Composition et Perception," March 1987, Geneva, Switzerland.

kinds of structure he imagined might overcome this gap, but I would be among the first to explore them if they could be identified.

Beneath the stylistic objection lies a philosophical issue that I think is the ultimate cause of the antagonism toward my article. The progressive-modernist aesthetic emerged in the nineteenth century out of a Hegelian framework in which cultural development was viewed in terms of dialectical historical forces. Significance was ascribed to an artist who could bring this ineluctable process to the next stage. Composers who saw themselves in this light made self-serving statements in the name of history, such as Schoenberg's remark that the invention of the 12-tone method assured the supremacy of German music for the next hundred years (Stuckenschmidt 1978), and Boulez's (1991, 113) assertion that any composer who has not experienced the necessity of serialism is useless. Many lesser figures have continued this kind of rhetoric. The heady mantle of prophet and historical arbiter removes the artist from common bonds and licenses the refusal of limits that are not self-imposed. An artist in this mindset is compelled to embrace a tabula rasa view of human nature, for only then is he or she completely free to announce a new order of things. Babbitt (2003, 78–85, 466–87) adopted this philosophical position through his alignment with the school of logical positivism, but it is implied by any composer who promotes a new compositional procedure on the basis of its alleged historical necessity.

CCCS undermines this view by its view that there is more to human nature than learning by association, that there is a capacity for music that incorporates propensities and mental representations of the kinds discussed in chapters 2 and 3. A progressive modernist may dismiss this view as retro, but it is unexceptional from the perspective of the biological and cognitive sciences. Science does not see culture as unmoored from nature. To turn the tables on historical one-upmanship, I find myself in a twenty-first-century position confronting a nineteenth-century ideology.

Since this discussion has effectively entered the realm of politics, let me take the argument a step further and observe that the progressive-modernist aesthetic grew out of the same intellectual milieu as Marxist-Leninist thought. I do not suggest a facile correlation between art and politics. Indeed, many radical poets and composers in the early twentieth century were right wing, and Stalin was hardly a friend of artistic modernism. What is interesting, rather, is that the progressive-modernist aesthetic shares structural features with Marxist-Leninism: submission to inexorable historical forces that unfold in a linear progression, allegiance to prophets who foretell and assist this progression, and a view of human nature stripped of nature and made completely malleable by these historical forces. Given such parallels, one might conclude that with the fall of communism this aesthetic would also decline. Perhaps it has, but it has extraordinary staying power, in part because state funding (at least in Europe) has allowed it to perpetuate relatively untouched by larger political and economic pressures. A deeper reason for its endurance is that it lends assurance in an age that lacks consensus about musical standards. If values are in doubt, one can at least rely on innovation. The broader culture's emphasis on technological innovation reinforces this view. Nor has there been a vigorous alternative to compete with it. By turning to the cognitive science of music instead of historical progressivism as a musical foundation, CCCS sought to outline the beginnings of such an alternative.

It would be a misunderstanding to conclude from this discussion that I oppose innovation. On the contrary, I welcome it, although I see it as a lesser value than the more elusive concept of originality. But I have little interest in innovation that ignores the structures and limits of the musical mind. The kind of innovation that I care about respects, takes advantage of, and even stretches these structures and limits. Let us return to the themes of CCCS in this spirit.

The distinction between complexity and complicatedness can be enriched if cast along the two axes in figure 4.2. The horizontal axis represents depth of inferred hierarchy, and the vertical axis represents density of a musical surface in terms of the number and nonredundancy of events per unit time. A composition fits somewhere in the four

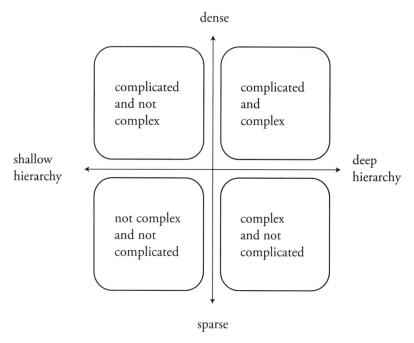

dense

complicated
and not
complex

complicated
and
complex

shallow
hierarchy

deep
hierarchy

not complex
and not
complicated

complex
and not
complicated

sparse

Figure 4.2. Complexity and complicatedness in four quadrants.

quadrants. For example, the Schubert *Moment Musical* discussed in chapter 2 has an uncomplicated surface yet is complex, so it belongs in the southeast quadrant. Boulez's *Marteau* is complicated but not complex and belongs in the northwest quadrant. A typical minimalist piece is neither complex nor complicated and fits in the southwest quadrant. Most pieces by Bach or Schoenberg are both complicated and complex and fit in the northeast quadrant.

This typology is approximate. A piece often moves from one quadrant to another as its form evolves; besides, its categorization changes depending on the musical dimensions under consideration. The passage from Beethoven's Fifth Symphony discussed in chapter 3 (see figure 3.1) will illustrate. The surface of the music is motivically repetitive and uncomplicated. Its metrical structure has many hierarchical levels and hence is complex. Its grouping structure is also complex. Indeed,

Figure 4.3. Elliott Carter, Second String Quartet, bars 57–61.

its grouping pattern of 1 + 1 + 2 is recursively embedded. Each four-bar unit is 1 + 1 + 2; the continuation of the sentence (*Satz*) is 2 + 2 + 4 (bars 14–21); and the sentence as a whole is 4 + 4 + 8 (bars 6–21). Yet the harmony is not complex, comprising a simple alternation of tonic and dominant except for the predominant augmented sixth in bar 20.

Figure 4.3, from Carter's Second String Quartet, provides a contrast. The surface is complicated, though not especially so compared to many other passages in the work. The rhythms do not project meter, for the stresses at the surface do not coincide and reinforce one another. Instead, each instrument moves at its own tempo. The quintuplet sixteenths in the first violin correspond to metronome marking 560, five times the initial notated tempo of 112; the staccato chords in the second violin are at metronome marking 70, consistently so through the notated tempo modulations; the triplet eighths in the viola are at metronome marking 336; and the cello accelerates from metronome marking 74.7 to 186.7. The notational complication arises from the necessity to relate the four tempo streams to one another. At the same time, the independence of the four lines erases any composite grouping. Each instrument plays its own characteristic pitch intervals, rhythms, and gestures, but these relations are associative rather than hierarchical (to invoke a distinction from chapter 2). In short, this music has a fascinating surface that does not project hierarchy in any dimension. It is complicated but not complex.

This excerpt is characteristic of much contemporary music in its flat hierarchy and intricate, nonredundant surface. These features become still more pronounced in the music of "maximalist" composers and in music that engages varieties of noise. When listening to such music, one focuses on its sonic surface, as when gazing at a painting by Jackson Pollock. Like a Pollock, it gives a statistical impression. The statistical effect is a by-product of the absence of mental representation of structure. One listens on a textural rather than syntactic plane.

It will be useful at this point to shift the terminology of the discussion from complexity versus complicatedness to order versus disorder. "Order" is meant not in a sequential sense but as a feature of a musical passage that evokes cognitive representations. It is a more general term than "complexity"; it embraces not only the southeast and northeast quadrants of figure 4.2 but also the southwest quadrant. For example, much popular music is not complex, but it projects order. The Carter quartet is mostly dense and nonhierarchical and belongs in the northwest quadrant, but it is comparatively ordered in its associative structure. "Disorder" is meant not in a pejorative sense but as a feature of musical passage that does not evoke cognitive structures or does so only with difficulty. Order and disorder exist on a continuum.

CCCS argued in favor of order over disorder, but there is a more inclusive way to frame the issue. To begin with, it is possible to give order to music whose details sound disordered. Two ways to do this are, first, to juxtapose blocks of texture so that the blocks rather than individual events become the primary objects of heard structure, as in Xenakis's *Pithoprakta* and Ligeti's *Atmosphères;* and, second, to transform the surface from one textural state to another in a gradual linear process, as in minimalist phase pieces and some early spectral pieces. Juxtaposition of opposing textural blocks creates order through clear demarcation of large-scale groups. Linear process creates order by projecting a constant rate of change. There are other, more complex ways to harness disorder. The key insight is to realize that almost all music moves in some degree between order and disorder.

An example from the tonal repertory will illustrate. The exposition of Mozart's G minor Symphony closes in orderly fashion with a repeated dominant-to-tonic progression in the secondary key of **B**♭. The transition to the development, shown in figure 4.4a, suddenly veers to **f**♯ in a moment of radical disorder. One is temporarily lost in pitch space. At the parallel transition in the finale, there appears the equally disorienting passage shown in figure 4.4b. In both movements, a descending line in thirds in the woodwinds checks the moment of disorder, after which the principal themes, each with an extended anacrusis in the violins, reestablish order. Mozart composed order and disorder into the design of the symphony.

Ligeti's *Lontano* is an example of a complex nontonal work built from a mixture of order and disorder. Most of its texture grows out of small-interval pitch canons (the rhythms of the canonic unfolding are somewhat variable), producing linear processes that are partly predictable and partly statistical. Moments of sustained bare intervals periodically interrupt the dense canonic texture to punctuate the form into large-scale blocks. Figure 4.5 sketches the primary instances of these signposts. But even as they give global order to the form, they do not project order themselves, for they do not repeat or form a clear pattern. If they

(a)

(b)

Figure 4.4. Mozart, G minor Symphony, transition into development sections: (a) first movement, (b) fourth movement.

involved repetition—if, for instance, the opening unison on A♭ recurred later on—the listener would infer order by making a prolongational connection between the two and subsuming the intervening signposts in relation to them. If they progressed in a regular intervallic pattern, the listener would trace the orderly process. Through avoidance of repetition and pattern, the signposts mark an open-ended, nonhierarchical pitch-space journey. As the arrows in figure 4.5 suggest, one hears the signposts as a sequence without further structure.

The first section of Kurtag's piano piece *In Memoriam András Mihály* (later reworked as the third movement of the orchestral work *Stele*) provides a contrast to *Lontano*. It is built around several departures from and returns to the opening chord, creating a prolongational structure. Figure 4.6 shows the progression together with its prolongational and functional analyses. The first chord is designated RS for "referential sonority," a broader term than "tonic." The first departure is to a nonproximate neighbor in bar 2. In bars 3–4 there are departures and returns twice to chromatic neighboring chords, followed in bars 4–6 by an expansion of the nonproximate neighbor and a gradual return to the

Figure 4.5. Moments of stasis in Ligeti's *Lontano*. Rehearsal letters are indicated.

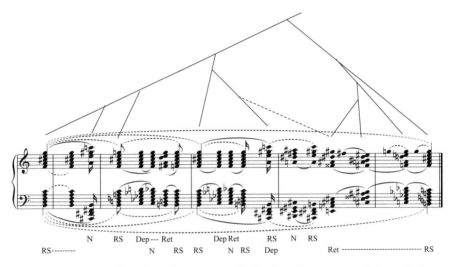

Figure 4.6. Prolongational and functional analysis of the first section of Kurtag's *In Memoriam András Mihály*. For clarity the tree shows only relatively global connections. Function designations: RS = referential sonority; N = neighbor (proximate or not); Dep = departure; Ret = return.

opening chord. In the second and third sections, which are not shown, the music departs entirely from the referential sonority and returns to a modified version of it, producing an ABA' global form.

The referential sonority is hierarchically superordinate not because of its stable position in a hierarchical pitch space but by virtue of its surface salience. I originally described reduction by salience in terms of atonal prolongational structure (Lerdahl 1989), in response to previous attempts to analyze atonal music from a Schenkerian perspective

(Salzer 1952; Travis 1966). Reduction by salience can be applied as well to tonal music. Indeed, a few of GTTM's preference rules for time-span reduction rely on salience. It seems odd to invoke salience as a primary factor in tonal reduction, however, because in Classical tonal syntax salience is relatively haphazard but stability is central. In highly chromatic music of the late nineteenth and early twentieth centuries, however, salience competes with stability because of the weakening of the tonal hierarchy. In genuinely atonal music, beginning with Schoenberg, salience fills the vacuum left by the absence of stability. (Chapters 7 and 8 of TPS trace this development in detail.)

Reduction by salience tends to be a fairly local phenomenon because of the lack of any mental schema to assist it. But if the following steps are taken, the resultant atonal prolongational sequences will have at least moderate hierarchical complexity. Let Z be the referential sonority, with progression backward on the alphabet signifying increasing tension and progression toward Z signifying decreasing tension:

(1) Construct degrees of harmonic identity, from full return of the same sonority to calibrated partial returns: $Z \rightarrow Z$, $Z \rightarrow Z'$.

(2) Build degrees of contrast through simple neighboring and passing motions between full and partial identities: $Z \rightarrow Y \rightarrow Z$, $Y \rightarrow X \rightarrow Y'$.

(3) Create patterns of increasing and decreasing tension: $X \rightarrow W \rightarrow V$, $V \rightarrow W \rightarrow X$.

(4) Establish a means of cadencing—that is, of creating resolution or closure at the end of a phrase or section. A standard cadence in most styles is formulaic and reduces tension in three stages: $X \rightarrow Y \rightarrow Z$.

(5) Combine these operations in sundry ways, beginning with normative schemas such as the bell-curve pattern of tension and relaxation that occurs in many musical idioms: $Z' \rightarrow Y \rightarrow V \rightarrow X \rightarrow Y \rightarrow Z$.

(6) Build larger nested patterns from (2), (3), (4), and (5) through basic operations of transposition, insertion, prefixing, and appending.

I first conceived the idea of reduction without stability not by ana-
lyzing atonal pitch structures but through an exploration of timbral
organization. While at IRCAM (Institut de Recherche et Coordination
Acoustique/Musique) in the mid-1980s, I was disturbed by the discrepancy between the reliance of spectral composers on timbre and the
universal lack of understanding of how to organize it. Inspired by conversations with David Wessel, I attempted, in spite of the usual view of
timbral relations as associative rather than hierarchical, to construct
timbral hierarchies (Lerdahl 1987). I employed the quasi-physical-
modeling vocal-synthesis program *Chant* (Rodet, Potard, and Barrière
1984) to generate vowels with fixed pitch and loudness in order to focus
exclusively on timbral variation. I discovered that in order to do anything interesting, at least two dimensions in vowel space were necessary. This was the beginning of my construction of musical spaces. I
also found that timbre is multidimensional in ways that are difficult to
measure. For example, timbral brightness (the perceptual correlate of
the averaged height and amplitude of the partials of a pitch) does not
easily compare to harmonicity (the degree to which partials correspond
to integer multiples of a fundamental). Moreover, unlike pitch space,
timbral dimensions are not circular but linear; they do not offer any
equivalent to the octave. Yet there is a place on each timbral line that is
psychoacoustically least tense (or least dissonant). Depending on the
timbral dimension, the least tense point is sometimes at one end of the
line, sometimes somewhere in the middle.

I sought a continuous timbral space and constructed, imperfectly,
the two-dimensional vowel space in figure 4.7 from two axes of brightness. On the vertical axis, /a/ (as in "father") is relaxed, /u/ (as in "foot")
is intermediate, and /i/ (as in "feet") is tense. The horizontal axis
increases tension within each category (through manipulation of third
formants). In both directions I created perceptually regular timbral
intervals—in itself a noteworthy result—and made short prolongational structures with neighboring and passing functions, such as
$/a_1/{\rightarrow}/u_1/{\rightarrow}/a_1/$ and $/u_1/{\rightarrow}/i_2/{\rightarrow}/u_3/$, respectively. These relations can

/i₁/ /i₂/ /i₃/

/u₁/ /u₂/ /u₃/

/a₁/ /a₂/ /a₃/

Figure 4.7. Timbre space made up of two axes of brightness and with equal intervals on each axis.

increasing brightness

transpose and invert. They can also embed recursively, as in the double-neighbor motion $/a_1/\rightarrow/u_1/\rightarrow/i_1/\rightarrow/u_1/\rightarrow/a_1/$. From these simple elements I built perceivably viable prolongational structures of up to twenty timbral events, taking steps along the lines of those listed above for atonal prolongational structures.

Although I succeeded in creating fragile timbral hierarchies, it was apparent that they would be perceptually overwhelmed by pitch relationships if placed in a less restricted musical context. Moreover, the timbral objects did not vary over time and hence were monotonous. Interesting timbres evolve, but in doing so their structural robustness diminishes. Despite its very qualified success, this project opened doors in my thinking and paved the way toward other fruitful developments.

Since then I have retreated from timbral hierarchies and sought to lend order to timbre through its interaction with other hierarchical components. In a Haydn symphony, for example, the horns, trumpets, and tympani are tuned to tonic and dominant pitches because they do not transpose (due to the absence of valves and pedals at the time). Accordingly, when these instruments play, they orient the listener to the chief harmonic pillars within the tonal idiom. To take a nontonal case, in Messiaen's *Chronochromie* the disposition of groups of instruments is highly distinctive and appears in fixed order in cycles of strophes and antistrophes. As a result, timbre is the primary carrier of the work's global grouping structure.

A preoccupation with timbre goes back at least to Berlioz and has grown to the present day. The more central timbre is to an aesthetic, the greater is its burden in providing perceptual order. The problem of timbral organization remains one of the great issues of contemporary music. It becomes still greater if, following the extended instrumental techniques pioneered by Lachenmann, noise is added to the timbral repertoire. Noise is nonpitched randomly fluctuating timbre. It lacks the coherent timbral dimensions of brightness, harmonicity, vibrato, and so forth, and consequently it permits only coarse classification (as in Schaeffer 1966). Noise takes on order only in cooperation with more structural components. If, for example, a series of phrases ends in wood-like sounds, these sounds can act as an approximate timbral rhyme to articulate the grouping structure.

Perhaps the turn to noise among many young composers is a reaction to the sense of futility of what to do with pitch. I can well understand this reaction, for, as reported in chapter 1, when I was young I went through a similar struggle when I tried to transfer form-bearing structure from pitch to rhythm and timbre. Many composers find themselves caught between flight from past musical materials and the incapacity of new materials to project perceivable form. As a result, many of them give up altogether on the search for an intelligible musical syntax.[5]

A more tractable issue in recent composition is the organization of microtonal tuning (tunings of pitches and intervals outside of the equal-tempered chromatic scale). How to select and organize microtones is a far from trivial issue. The situation is not like that of the turn from diatonic to chromatic harmony in the nineteenth century. Diatonic harmony was widely understood and schematized, so it was possible to

---

5. See McAdams (1989) for a broad review of form-bearing elements in music.

develop chromatic harmony on that foundation. There is much less agreement about the principles and practice of atonal harmony built from the equal-tempered scale. As a result, equal-tempered atonal harmony provides little basis for the systematic development of microtonal harmony.

One route, explored in the twentieth century by a number of composers, is to divide the octave into equal divisions other than 12. Another is to employ intervals from the natural harmonic series. In the 1980s, some composers derived microtones by sidebands in frequency modulation, in imitation of timbres produced on Yamaha synthesizers. Many contemporary composers have recorded *musique concrète* sounds—say, a fork on a glass, thunder, or Tibetan bells—and converted their spectral analyses into notated harmonies. These approaches are ad hoc and unsystematic.

From the perspective of CCCS, one way to proceed is to add a microtonal level to the basic space, thus placing microtones in a hierarchical framework. Figure 4.8a does this with quarter tones at the bottom level of the basic space. The orientation to a C major chord in C major is a placeholder for what could be any number of basic-space contexts. To represent different tunings conveniently, figure 4.8b converts the numbers in figure 4.8a into cents. Figure 4.8c alters figure 4.8b with justly tuned intervals; other tunings are of course possible. The bottom level in figure 4.8c leaves further microtonal nuances unspecified since the particulars are likely to vary according to context.

The expanded basic space in figure 4.8 offers a hierarchical format within which to represent and explore microtonal melodic nuance. Expressive microtones in North Indian ragas, for instance, often occur as neighboring or passing embellishments of diatonic scale degrees that are tuned in relation to justly tuned octaves and fifths. Performers of Turkish *makam* modify the tuning of leading tones—as do Classical Western performers—so that they are closer to, hence more attracted to, adjacent stable tones (Cetiz 2017).

(a)

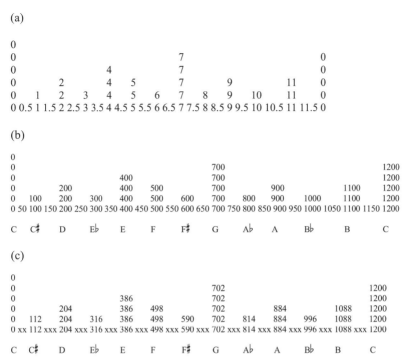

0
0
0
0
0
0

```
0
0                               7                     0
0                 4             7                     0
0        2        4    5        7        9        11  0
0    1   2   3    4    5    6   7    8   9   10   11  0
0 0.5 1 1.5 2 2.5 3 3.5 4 4.5 5 5.5 6 6.5 7 7.5 8 8.5 9 9.5 10 10.5 11 11.5 0
```

(b)

```
0
0                                700                              1200
0                   400          700                             1200
0         200       400   500    700        900          1100    1200
0   100   200  300  400   500 600 700  800  900  1000    1100    1200
0 50 100 150 200 250 300 350 400 450 500 550 600 650 700 750 800 850 900 950 1000 1050 1100 1150 1200
```

C   C♯   D   E♭   E   F   F♯   G   A♭   A   B♭   B   C

(c)

```
0
0                                702                              1200
0                   386          702                             1200
0         204       386   498    702        884          1088    1200
0   112   204  316  386   498 590 702  814  884  996     1088    1200
0 xx 112 xxx 204 xxx 316 xxx 386 xxx 498 xxx 590 xxx 702 xxx 814 xxx 884 xxx 996 xxx 1088 xxx 1200
```

C   C♯   D   E♭   E   F   F♯   G   A♭   A   B♭   B   C

Figure 4.8. Addition of microtonal levels to the basic space, which is oriented to I/**C** as a default: (a) quarter-tone space notated in pitch-class notation; (b) quarter-tone space in cents; (c) justly tuned space in cents, with the microtonal level left unspecified.

An advantage of a basic-space approach to microtones is that it alleviates the problem of micro-mistuning. Tuning in practice, as opposed to in theory, is approximate in all musical styles because of human limitations in accuracy of sound production. If microtones are cut too finely, they demand accuracy to an unrealistic degree. If placed in a basic-space context, however, they have a location that is interpretable in the more stable context of the next level up in the basic space.

Much recent music has avoided a basic-space hierarchical framework for microtonal melodies, presumably because of the historical and

Figure 4.9. Microtonal melodic lines at the beginning of the first song of Grisey's *Quatre chants pour franchir le seuil.*

cultural associations evoked by such an approach. For a different approach, consider the microtonal lines in the first song of Grisey's *Quatre chants pour franchir le seuil.* Figure 4.9 shows the three contrapuntal lines in the opening measures; this texture continues throughout most of the song. The lines derive not from a hierarchical pitch space but from mostly adjacent partials in the harmonic series (Hervé 2009; Macklay 2014). Adjacent movement among lower partials yields a triadic arpeggio, but among higher partials it creates scalelike patterns that mimic stepwise melodic motion. The melodic counterpoint in entire sections of the song derives from a single fundamental. When the fundamental changes, the lines modulate. As the music progresses, the lines with smaller intervals become higher and those with larger intervals become lower, in correspondence with the harmonic series, producing a kind of vertical hierarchy. But because the fundamental is implied rather than stated and many of the partials are very high and often octave-displaced, the perceptual orientation of the pitches is perched on the edge of disorder. That the three lines are in a tempo ratio of 3:4:5 increases the sense of disorder. Most of the order comes instead from saturated motivic repetition of the opening material.

Microtonal harmony presents somewhat different issues than does microtonal melody. Spectral composers in particular employ an arsenal of technological means with which to generate microtonal harmonies— frequency modulation, spectral analysis and resynthesis, expansion

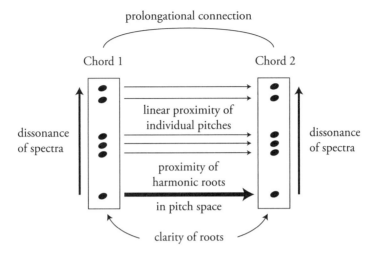

Figure 4.10. Structural factors in microtonal harmonic progression.

or compression of the harmonic spectrum, spectral interpolation, frequency distortion, formant manipulation, and so forth—but there has been comparatively little discussion of how to organize the resulting harmonies.[6] On the one hand, I regard the spectral vision of creating musical form out of sound itself to be one of the really fertile ideas in music of the last half century. On the other hand, there is a gap between the spectral ideal and the resultant forms. The link from sound to form is weak.

There are ways nonetheless to lend structural order to microtonal harmony. Assume the two microtonal chords represented schematically in figure 4.10. The white rectangles are chords, and the black circles inside them are individual pitches of the chords. The overall proximity of the two chords can be computed as the weighted sum of three factors: (1) the linear proximity in voice leading between the two chords; (2) the relative psychoacoustic root clarity of each of the two chords; (3) the proximity of their roots.

6. Murail (2005) is representative in this regard.

The first factor is calculated as the minimum log-frequency distance among pitches in the two chords. Figure 4.10 represents this factor graphically by thin arrows: the more horizontal the arrows, the more proximate the voice leading. The second factor, root clarity, depends on the degree to which pitches in a chord fit the template of the natural harmonic series (Terhardt 1984). For instance, the most rooted chord is a major triad, the root of a minor triad is slightly ambiguous, and the root of the chord C4-F♯4-B4 is quite ambiguous.

The thick arrow in figure 4.10 stands for the potentially strong third factor of root proximity. If the tonal case is any guide, root proximity is a matter not of log-frequency distance but of proximity in pitch space. In diatonic music, root proximity is measured by the number of steps taken on the cycle of fifths from one triad to the next, in octatonic music by steps on the cycle of minor thirds, and so on. If the microtonal chords in question are harmonic, the cycle of fifths and, secondarily, the cycle of major thirds are applicable because of the psychoacoustic prominence of the third partial and the secondary prominence of the fifth partial. Distances in just-intonation harmonic space then take the shape of the *Tonnetz* that has played such a prominent role in the history of music theory, from Euler (1739) through Oettingen (1866) and Riemann (1882) to present-day neo-Riemannian theory (Gollin and Rehding 2011). But if chords are inharmonic in some other way, another measure would apply. In constructing a pitch space for microtonal harmony, it makes strategic sense to begin with justly tuned microtonal chords and their resultant root distances before confronting root distances in other microtonal tunings. At the same time, because inharmonic chords that are not justly tuned have relatively ambiguous roots, root distance for these chords becomes a lesser factor in the overall equation.[7]

7. There is an interesting technical literature that bears on these and related issues of microtonal harmony, for example, Gilmore 1995; Hasegawa 2009; Sabat 2016.

Harmonic progression can take place not only from one chord to the next but also up and down the spectrum within a single sonority, as discussed for the melodic lines in *Quatre chants*. Although this notion is foreign to most tonal music, it is a vital factor in jazz, in which a particular chord function can include a variety of added or substituted pitches. This factor suggests another pitch-space dimension to harmony beyond what was explored in TPS.

Microtonal harmonies require prolongational structure, as represented by the slur at the top of figure 4.10, if they are to project order with any complexity. This aspect of musical organization has been absent in the spectral tradition. It can be developed not only through patterns of repetition but also through patterns of psychoacoustic tension. The issue of psychoacoustic tension in microtonal harmony connects conceptually with my timbral study, for in a given timbral dimension there is a point of maximal relaxation and degrees of tension in relation to it. Lerdahl and Krumhansl (2007) found that intuitions of tonal tension and relaxation are strong and consistent in a variety of circumstances. It seems reasonable to suppose that these intuitions will pertain to other musical contexts.[8]

Attempts to give order to atonality, timbre, noise, and microtones do not take place in a vacuum but engage with the nature of the materials themselves. In this connection, Babbitt (2003, 274–77) invoked four psychophysical scales of measurement (Stevens 1946) when arguing for the primacy of pitch among musical dimensions. In order of complexity, the scales are:

(1) A nominal scale that differentiates items qualitatively by category;

(2) An ordinal scale that places items in a rank order without quantifying their degrees of difference;

---

8. Pressnitzer and colleagues (2000) conducted an empirical study to explore the possibility of psychoacoustic tension and relaxation as a means of projecting structure in a microtonal context. I would hope to see more research of this kind.

(3) An interval scale that quantifies degrees of difference among items;

(4) A ratio scale that quantifies degrees of difference among items in relation to a nonarbitrary point of reference.

Noise belongs to a nominal scale. Room acoustics permits an ordinal scale with respect to distance and direction, but further quantification is not feasible despite the efforts of some electronic composers to send sound around from speaker to speaker in a structured manner. Dynamics belong to an ordinal scale. In the 1950s, several composers tried to convert dynamics to an interval scale in a vain attempt to extend serial thinking to that musical dimension. Timbral categories typically belong to a nominal scale, but within a category a given timbral dimension projects an ordinal scale. My study of timbral hierarchies showed that, under limited conditions, a timbral dimension is able to project an interval scale and even a ratio scale, since along any timbral dimension there is a psychophysical point of minimal dissonance. Rhythm in its various aspects fits an interval scale. If it permits the inference of a metrical grid, however, it projects a ratio scale. Pitch in an atonal idiom belongs to an interval scale, but in a tonal idiom it belongs to a ratio scale.

I agree with Babbitt on the primacy of pitch (and rhythm). The other musical dimensions are intrinsically more limited in the degree of structure they can project. They do not allow enough distinctions. The stasis that has overtaken contemporary music in the last half century is a consequence not only of rigid aesthetic views but also, more deeply, of the recalcitrance of the materials that composers have felt compelled to work with. It is challenging to lend order to rhythms that do not project meter and pitches that do not project hierarchy. It is astronomically more difficult to give order to timbre and noise. As I have argued, however, timbre and noise can achieve a degree of order if placed in patterned ways with hierarchical structures.

CHAPTER FIVE

From Theory to Composition

One approach to understanding Boulez's music is to study its compositional grammar, beginning with partitions of a 12-tone row, proceeding to the construction of pitch domains by "multiplication" of pairs of the partitions, and identifying the unordered presentation of the contents of the domains in an actual piece (Boulez 1971; Koblyakov 1993). One can go on to describe these procedures using pitch-class set theory and situate them with respect to related approaches by earlier composers (Heinemann 1998).

Another approach is to develop a listening grammar. I can imagine two promising approaches. First, Boulez's post-*Marteau* music often dwells on proliferations within static harmonies, so it should be illuminating to analyze it from the perspective of atonal prolongational theory (see figure 4.6 and Lerdahl 2001b, chapter 8). Second, his harmonies tend to sound alike. They typically have four to seven pitches. They avoid strongly consonant octaves and fifths and the roughness of minor seconds in favor of moderate dissonance produced by combinations of major seconds, thirds (or sixths), fourths, tritones, and sevenths, spaced fairly closely but not crunched together. These features could be described by a constraint system based on degrees of sensory dissonance. I can attest personally that Boulez had no interest in

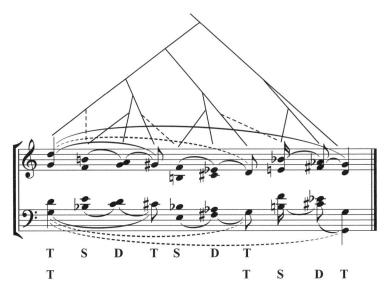

Figure 5.1. Prolongational analysis of variation 6 of the First Quartet (from figure 1.9).

Schenkerian prolongational theory, and I doubt that he studied the psychoacoustic literature on sensory dissonance. In considering an appropriate listening as opposed to compositional grammar, a composer's predilections may not be germane.

My own case is different from that of Boulez and many other composers, for my intent is to base the compositional grammar on the listening grammar—that is, my compositional methods on principles of musical cognition. My understanding of musical cognition is germane to how I compose.

Consider again the syntax of the beginning of my First String Quartet discussed in chapter 1. Figure 5.1 repeats the prolongational analysis of variation 6 from figure 1.9. I shall review eleven features that the syntax embodies. The crucial point about them is that they are all grounded in perceptual and cognitive principles.

First and foremost is the principle of elaboration. This passage is heard in a hierarchical fashion, as represented by the tree and slurs in figure 5.1. Second, and as a consequence of the first, the music is oriented toward a pitch center, the dominating structure of the event hierarchy. Traditionally, a point of orientation is called the tonic, but depending on context it might be referred to as the referential sonority. In figure 5.1 the tonic is **G.** A third feature is that the listener infers event hierarchies not from pitch alone but from a combination of pitch and rhythmic features. Figure 5.1 does not show this derivation, but GTTM explains how it works by its stages of time-span segmentation and reduction, and TPS extends the procedure to chromatic and atonal idioms in ways that accommodate this particular analysis. A fourth feature is that sensory consonance and dissonance drive the syntax, here through progressions from dissonant chords with minor seconds and tritones to intermediate chords with major seconds and fifths to consonant chords in open fifths. As discussed in chapter 1, this feature does not play a role in common-practice tonal syntax except in the treatment of nonharmonic tones, but it is central in various other musical idioms.

A fifth feature, the principle of attraction, comes from the schema of a basic space, as discussed in chapter 2; the space causes unstable pitches and chords to gravitate toward proximate stable pitches and chords. The quartet syntax embodies this feature in its proximate voice leading in all four voices, in coordination with degrees of sensory consonance but without reinforcement from a coherent basic space. A sixth feature, harmonic functionality, is an emergent property of a prolongational event hierarchy, as mentioned in chapter 2. A seventh feature, not shown in figure 5.1 but apparent in many later passages in the First Quartet, is that harmonic functions can elaborate vertically. By way of illustration, the cadential progression in figure 5.2a elaborates by addition in 5.2b, subtraction in 5.2c, and substitution in 5.2d.

How much alteration can a harmony undergo without losing its particular function? In a tonal context, functional identity depends in part on pitch-space distance measured from a point of orientation. In a chord progression X→Y→Z, for example, if Z is the point of orientation, X assumes an S-function if it is farther away from Z than Y is. If it is closer

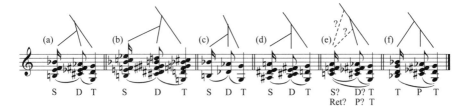

Figure 5.2. Harmonic functions: (a) the closing cadential progression from figure 5.1; (b) addition of pitches; (c) subtraction of pitches; (d) substitution of pitches (in this case, by transposition); (e) ambiguous functionality resulting from an unclear progression in terms of sensory consonance and dissonance; (f) definite passing function for the second chord.

than Y, its prolongational connection yields a function other than S. In an atonal context, distance is measured not in a schematic pitch space but by pitch-class and interval-class commonality (see Lerdahl 2001b, chapter 8). For the quartet syntax, there is an additional factor, sensory consonance and dissonance. In the sequence X→Y→Z with Z most consonant, X tends to function as S if it is more dissonant than Y. If X has about the same degree of consonance as Y, as in the first two chords in figure 5.2e, its function is ambiguous; it might instead connect directly to Z, turning Y into a passing function. If X closely resembles Z, as in figure 5.2f, in which the roots of the first and third chords are the same, it assumes T-function, and Y definitely has a passing function.

An eighth feature of the quartet syntax has its source not in music but in general physical behavior: the tendency to relax into closure to terminate a unified action. In most musical idioms, closure takes the form of a formulaic cadence at the end of a phrase or section. (An extra-terrestrial trying to decipher a human musical idiom would do well to look at its cadences, for how it achieves closure tells a great deal about how its overall syntax works.) A ninth feature, nested self-similarity, follows from the eighth, for formulaic cadences repeat at multiple levels of a grouping hierarchy. Both of these features are evident in figure 5.1. A tenth feature is again beyond music per se: the tendency toward

Figure 5.3. Approximate tension curve for the progression in figure 5.1.

symmetry or near-symmetry as an organizing force. In figure 5.1 the voice leading in the final cadence is fully symmetrical, and so is the subordinate cadence on **C♯** in relation to the tonic. However, the axes of symmetrical voice leading, G and D, divide the octave not in half but nearly in half, producing near-symmetry. The quartet syntax plays with this distinction, sometimes substituting the near-symmetry of the perfect fifth for the symmetry of the tritone, or vice versa.[1]

An eleventh feature, the projection of patterns of tension and relaxation, arises from a combination of a prolongational event hierarchy (feature one), a schematic and hierarchical pitch space, sensory dissonance (feature four), and attractions (feature five). Figure 5.3 gives a slightly elaborated version of figure 5.1 and substitutes an approximate tension curve for the prolongational tree. The curve is approximate because, unlike the tonal case, I have not found a quantitative means of calculating tension for this syntax. Intuitions of relative tension nonetheless remain strong, and they involve a wider range of musical dimensions

1. In this connection, the basilar membrane in the inner ear converts frequency distance into ratio distance. The distinction between the two can be expressed by arithmetic and geometric means. Given two pitches in Hz, M and N, their arithmetic mean $A = (M + N)/2$. Their geometric mean R is $R/M = N/R$. Thus $R^2 = M*N$ and $R = \sqrt{(M*N)}$. If M and N are an octave apart, say $M = 200$ Hz and $N = 400$ Hz, $A = (200 + 400)/2 = 300$ Hz, forming a perfect fifth above M and a perfect fourth below N (ratios of 3/2 and 4/3). $R = \sqrt{(200*400)} = 283$ Hz, forming a tritone both above M and below N (283/200 = 400/283). A is the midpoint between M and N in terms of Hz, and R is the midpoint in terms of ratio.

than does the model of tonal tension reviewed in chapter 2. I regard patterns of tension and relaxation as fundamental to musical expression.[2]

Missing from the list of eleven features, and therefore from the treatment of tension, is a coherent pitch space. Chapter 6 of TPS develops a number of nondiatonic basic spaces along with their spatial projections and slots them into a matrix of cognitive-structural features. The number of features that a basic space has measures its degree of coherence. The quartet syntax does not possess many of these features. Figure 5.4a repeats the syntax's cadential progression, here oriented to **C.** The bottom level gives the chromatic scale, but what is the second or scale level? A coherent basic space at a given level has about half the number of elements as does the level immediately beneath it. If all the pitch classes in the progression are included, as in figure 5.4b, ten of the twelve chromatic pitch classes appear at level 2. If the final chord is represented, level 3 has only two pitch classes. This is not a preferred basic space. Moreover, ten of twelve pitches are too many to separate level 2 effectively from level 1. Without an operative level 2, there is no intermediate level between chords and the total chromatic, and the distinction between chord and key collapses. In addition, because there are three chord types, the syntax weakens any distinction between harmonic and nonharmonic tones. Finally, since the chord types are different, a spatial projection of level 3 is problematic. One solution is to build on distances from the resolution on open fifths, yielding a simple cycle of fifths. A second solution, which the quartet syntax opts for, is based on the root of the second chord and symmetrical division of the octave by a tritone. Later on in the piece, the tritone further divides into the cycle of minor thirds. Under either solution, the materials themselves impede a robust multidimensional pitch space.

Another limitation of the quartet syntax is that, unlike diatonic tonality, it does not easily accommodate just intonation. It is built on

2. The representation of harmonic progression by a tension curve and the incorporation of dissonance as a driver of musical syntax are reminiscent of Hindemith's ([1937] 1942) treatment of "harmonic fluctuation." Hindemith, however, had little notion of prolongational structure.

(a)

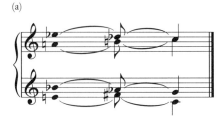

(b)

Level 4: C   (C)
Level 3: C   G   (C)
Level 2: C C♯   D♯ E   F♯ G G♯ A B♭ B (C)
Level 1: C C♯ D D♯ E F F♯ G G♯ A B♭ B (C)

Figure 5.4. The basic space and the First Quartet's cadential progression: (a) the progression, (b) the pitches of all three chords cast in basic-space format.

the 12-equal-tempered scale. This restricts its range of microtonal possibilities.

The form of the First Quartet builds by expanding variations, as discussed in chapter 1. Each successive variation is about three halves the length of the previous one. Figure 5.1 is a prolongational snapshot early in this process. As the variations become longer and more complicated, they differentiate internally into sections of increasingly contrasting character, like an embryo growing into different body parts. The labeled groups beneath the reduction in figure 5.5 give a rough idea of the character of the emerging sections within a variation. The opening G chord acts as an introduction to a double exposition. The first half of the exposition moves down the minor-third cycle to cadence on **C♯,** and the second continues the cycle to **G,** closing off the variation's first and larger half. The second half has a slower underlying harmonic rhythm. It begins with a whirlwind presto built from arpeggiation of the S-functioning chord and gradually subsides, in a more lyrical section supported by the D-functioning chord, into closure and a coda centered on **G.**

Because of the geometric expansion, the last two of fifteen variations occupy almost half of the piece—about four and six minutes,

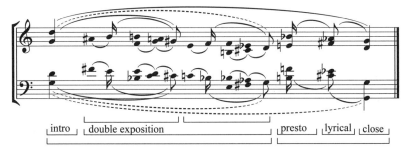

Figure 5.5. Differentiated sections in the First Quartet's expanding variations.

respectively. In the course of the expansion, the syntax gradually loosens but returns into focus at structural joints. The loosening is my response to the absence of an adequate basic space and the resulting limit in distinctions that the syntax can afford. Stepping outside the syntax broadens the First Quartet's stylistic range. The situation somewhat resembles that of a jazz musician who improvises outside the standard blues progression and returns to it.

The syntactic loosening is also a response to my psychological and expressive need to engage and control disorder. As discussed in chapter 4, I view the interaction of order and disorder as an indispensable compositional resource. The interaction takes place over multiple musical dimensions. Figure 5.6 illustrates with eight dimensions. The center is the point of maximal stability. Motion along a given arrow away from the center increases disorder in that dimension, and motion toward the center increases order. It is essential to this conception that the endpoints of an arrow represent perceptual extremes in its dimension. For instance, the arrow for pitch consonance and dissonance has strong consonance at one end and strong dissonance at the other. If the arrow is short—if, for instance, the style stays within a small range of moderate dissonance, as in much of Boulez—motion along it projects less contrast and hence fewer distinctions.

Arrows can combine to intensify a progression toward order or disorder. Figure 5.7a shows a passage from the First Quartet's 13th variation

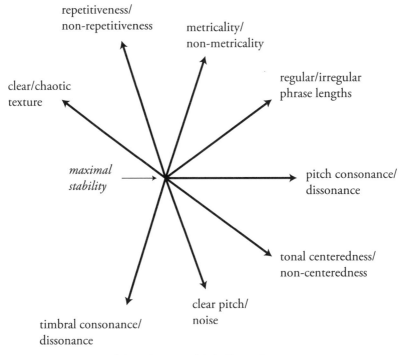

Figure 5.6. Order and disorder in multiple dimensions.

that begins outside the syntax and cadences with an S→D→T progression to **C♯**. (In terms of the expansion process, figure 5.7a realizes the cadential progression to **C♯** at the end of the first exposition in figure 5.5.) Three dimensions together bring the progression from disorder to order: comparative nonmetricality to metricality, pitch dissonance to consonance, and tonal noncenteredness to centeredness. The effect is one of tension followed by quick relaxation. Figure 5.7b gives the ending of the First Quartet. The passage cites the Quartet's opening progression and gradually dissipates into disorder in four dimensions acting jointly: metricality/nonmetricality, tonal centeredness/noncenteredness, clear pitch /noise, and timbral consonance/dissonance.

While composing the First Quartet, I conceived the idea of a three-quartet cycle—a Second Quartet to add two more expanding variations

(a)

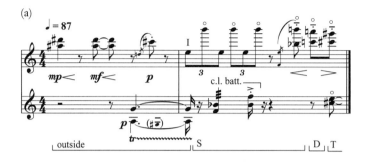

(b)

Figure 5.7. Order and disorder in the First Quartet: (a) cadence on C♯ in the 13th variation, (b) final measures of the piece.

of approximately nine and fourteen minutes in length, and a Third Quartet to consist of a single final variation of about twenty-two minutes. After many interruptions, I completed this design in 2010. The three pieces exist both independently and as three movements of a single seventy-minute work. The cycle as a whole is a huge manifestation

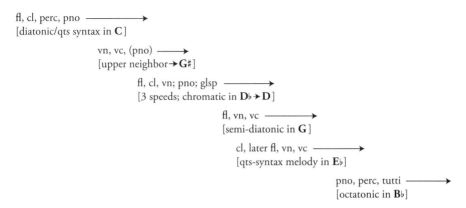

fl, cl, perc, pno ⟶
[diatonic/qts syntax in **C**]

    vn, vc, (pno) ⟶
    [upper neighbor→**G♯**]

        fl, cl, vn; pno; glsp ⟶
        [3 speeds; chromatic in **D♭**→**D**]

            fl, vn, vc ⟶
            [semi-diatonic in **G**]

                cl, later fl, vn, vc ⟶
                [qts-syntax melody in **E♭**]

                        pno, perc, tutti ⟶
                        [octatonic in **B♭**]

Figure 5.8. Overlapping expanding etudes in the first half of *Fantasy Etudes*.

of the principle of elaboration built on the foundation of a cognitively grounded syntax.

I think of a particular cognitive compositional grammar as a location in a space of options. A choice of a grammar yields formal and cognitive advantages and disadvantages. It is important to recognize both, for only then is one equipped to navigate the terrain of possibilities. This way of thinking led me, not long after completing an early version of the Second Quartet, to search for voice-leading and harmonic syntaxes other than the one employed in the string quartets. I embarked again on expanding variations, this time not as a unitary process as in the quartets but as multiple, overlapping perceptual streams. Each stream would explore a different syntactic pattern. The first piece to carry out this idea was *Fantasy Etudes* (1985), for mixed sextet. The "etude" part of the title refers to the syntactic study that constitutes each variation stream, the "fantasy" part to the sense of caprice that the contrasting streams create when juxtaposed.

Figure 5.8 sketches the streams of the first six expanding variations of *Fantasy Etudes*. The first etude mixes diatonic elements with the quartet syntax. The second etude develops a leading-tone idea from A to **G♯,** and the third works out chromatic neighboring chords around **D♭**

at three simultaneous speeds, eventually modulating the progression up a semitone. The fairly diatonic fourth etude, centered on **G,** is overlaid with the fifth etude, a long chromatic melody focusing on an attraction field oriented to **E♭**. The sixth etude grows from octatonic flourishes over low **B♭**. As this description suggests, the pitch structure in *Fantasy Etudes* modulates from stream to stream in two ways, by pitch center and by hypermodulation—that is, modulation between pitch spaces (see the discussion in chapter 3). The fourth etude is centered on **G** in diatonic space, the fifth on **E♭** in the space of the quartet syntax, and the sixth on **B♭** in octatonic space.

Fantasy Etudes attains unity not from its heterogeneous material but from the uniformity of the spiral technique that all the streams employ. In a sense, it is a process piece, albeit a very syntactic one compared to minimalist or spectral processes. The extent to which streams overlap varies, and the degree of textural density from overlapping streams becomes a factor in the evolving form. Crucial to the dramatic as well as formal impact of the multiple-stream technique is how far the streams separate perceptually. I took care to superimpose streams with strongly contrasting instrumentation, register, and figuration.

Given two hierarchically dominating events, an expanding variation can elaborate in three places: before the first dominating event as a prefix; between the two dominating events as an infix; or after the second dominating event as a suffix (to adapt terms from linguistic morphology). These options exist at multiple levels of structure. Elaboration by infix, since it takes place between two contextually stable points, creates a tensing-relaxing curve. The passages from the First Quartet in figures 1.8 and 1.9 expand by infixes. A prefix creates a sense of structural anacrusis and a suffix a sense of coda. Figure 5.9 illustrates prefixes and suffixes in variations 4–8 of the first etude of *Fantasy Etudes*. Progressively elaborated prefixes lead into the stable fifth C-G, and corresponding suffixes spin out from the cadences on unison C5. (The music between the pillars of C-G and the cadence in **C**—that is, its elaborations by infixes—is not shown.)

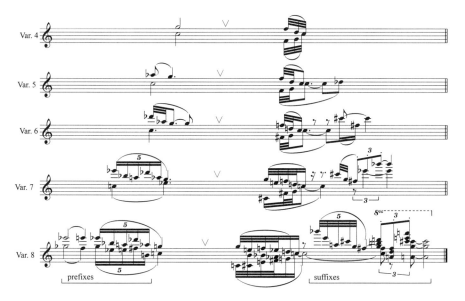

Figure 5.9. Progressive elaboration by prefixes and suffixes in the variations 4–8 of the first etude of *Fantasy Etudes*.

Not only harmonic progressions but also single lines can give rise to prolongations and functions. Figure 5.10a illustrates with the first five expanding variations of the fifth etude of *Fantasy Etudes,* a long melody in the clarinet. Figure 5.10b gives its basic-space framework, based on the quartet syntax. Figure 5.10c transposes the cadential progression in figure 5.2a to E♭ to show implicit functions of individual pitches in this context. Figure 5.10d gives the resulting prolongational and functional analysis. B♭–E♭ provide the T-function frame, the pitches A, E, and D assume D-function, and G and F♯ take on S-function. In the last two variations, the final E♭ is approached with strong semitone attractions, in the process flipping the hierarchical relationship between pitches A and E.

Much musical thought over the past century has dealt with pitch-class interval. One thinks of the 12-tone system and pitch-class set theory but also of Boulez's domains, George Perle's (1991) compositional system, or Carter's (2002) harmony catalog. The notion of music as just

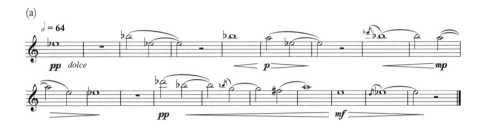

(a)

(b)

Eb
Eb   Bb
(C) Db D Eb E   F♯ G   A Bb B
  C Db D Eb E F F♯ G Ab A Bb B

(c)

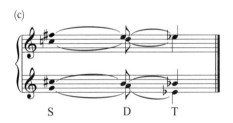

(d)

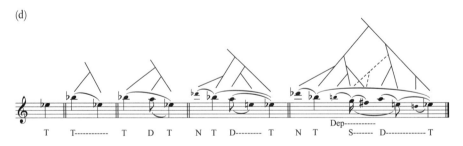

Figure 5.10. Prolongations, attractions, and functions in a single melodic line: (a) the first five expanding variations of the fifth etude of *Fantasy Etudes;* (b) the basic-space configuration of the melody; (c) the cadential progression, transposed to E♭, of the syntax of the string quartets; (d) the melody's prolongational and functional analysis.

a bunch of pitch-class intervals depresses me. In my view, at least as important as the intervals are the forces exerted on them. I seek to create musical contexts in which such forces are able to operate strongly. The melody in figure 5.10a is representative in this regard.

The streaming approach to expanding variations reached its apogee in the orchestra piece *Quiet Music* (1994). That work also explores ambiguity in global pitch center. The idea came from Krumhansl's (1990) key-finding algorithm, which correlates the distribution of tone durations (the aggregated duration of each pitch class in a piece) with the tone profile of each major and minor key (the empirically derived stability of pitch classes in a key; see chapter 2). The algorithm's output yields percentages of tonal orientation. A work might be said to be, for instance, 45 percent in **C**, 30 percent in **G**, and 20 percent in **a**, with a residue of more distant keys. The algorithm does not recognize any aspect of musical syntax such as grouping structure, the order of events, the hierarchy of events, or cadences. In contrast, my method of finding the key by the shortest path (see chapter 2) incorporates all of these structures and arrives at a definite tonic orientation. To be in a key is to be at a superordinate location in pitch space with a vista overlooking other locations near and far. Tonic orientation in a tonally ambiguous piece is like the Necker cube or duck-rabbit visual illusions familiar in the gestalt and philosophical literature (Koffka 1935; Wittgenstein 1953): one can toggle between one perception and the other, but one does not perceive the music in two keys at the same time.[3]

At the time of *Quiet Music*, I had not yet formulated my approach to key finding and was intrigued by the notion of several tonic orientations. I set up the beginning of the piece so that it pointed toward three possible tonics, summarized in figure 5.11a.[4] As I composed, I did not

---

3. See Lerdahl (2015b) for a detailed analysis of a well-known case of this kind, the song "Im wunderschönen Monat Mai" from Schumann's *Dichterliebe*.

4. Incidentally, this opening refers, as if in a dream, to the climax of *Chords* (see figure 1.3). My music is filled with self-references, creating a quasi-semantic web of connections whose discussion lies outside the scope of this book.

Figure 5.11. Tonal ambiguity and resolution in *Quiet Music:* (a) sketch of the beginning, with three potential tonics, **D**, **B♭**, and **E**; (b) a passage toward the end in which the harmony is oriented toward **E** and the melody toward **D**; (c) a summary of the essential harmonic motion of the final section, in which D4 is first interpreted as the 15th partial over low E♭ and then reinterpreted as the root of a D major triad.

know for a long time—quite unusually for me—where the piece would finally arrive. Near the end, I wrote a bitonal passage, part of which is shown in skeletal form in figure 5.11b, in which the harmony is oriented to **e** and the melody to **d,** both employing the quartet syntax. I accomplished the final resolution to **D**, summarized in figure 5.11c, first by shifting the harmonic root from E to low E♭ so that the pitches above it, in particular central D4, sound like overtones, and then by reorienting D4 upward as the root of an acoustically spaced D major triad. (This is one of many instances in which spectral thinking has infiltrated my music.)

After finishing *Quiet Music,* I took a vacation from composing to write TPS. When I returned to composition, I found that I had lost interest in expanding variations by independent streaming. I was bothered by the lack of logic between streams as opposed to the systematic treatment within a stream; how I coordinated streams was only by intuition and ear. Moreover, the ways in which the music modulated from one pitch center to another across streams was not controlled by the technique. I also found that none of the alternative expanding-variation syntaxes that I had tried out in the streaming pieces attained the cognitive-structural interest either of the quartet syntax, with its hierarchical control of harmonic consonance and dissonance and its integrated

Figure 5.12. Two of three streams at the beginning of the first movement of *Time after Time.*

treatment of voice-leading attractions, or of the diatonic space to which I occasionally turned. Consequently, beginning with the chamber work *Time after Time* (2000), I focused anew on the quartet syntax. Now multiple streams appeared not as unrelated superimpositions but grew directly out of the process of linear expansion. To illustrate, figure 5.12 gives two of the three streams at the beginning of the first movement of *Time after Time.* The stream in the lower staff enters as a coloration of the stream in the upper staff, but as the variations expand it gradually drifts away into its own development. Eventually it disappears as other streams materialize out of the overall expansion.

The expansion process in the first movement of *Time after Time* proceeds by a variable ratio of approximately 1.5, as in the quartet cycle. The second movement expands by a constant golden ratio of 1.62 through Fibonacci numbers that count the number of beats in embedded time-span segments.[5] Figure 5.13 illustrates schematically with the

5. The golden ratio, whose use in architecture goes back to antiquity, is the proportion such that the small is to the large as the large is to the whole. The Fibonacci series 2, 3, 5, 8, 13, 21 ... converges on the golden ratio: $3/2$, $5/3$, $8/3$, $13/8$, $21/13$.... I first employed it in the chamber orchestra piece *Waves* (1988), which stands at a consonant extreme in my output. The Fibonacci expansion creates a distancing effect, making familiar musical materials seem strange. (Incidentally, I do not make grand claims about the

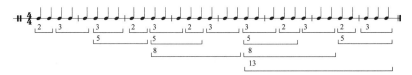

Figure 5.13. Schematic representation of embedded Fibonacci expansions in the second movement of *Time after Time*.

first five iterations of the expansion: 2 beats, then 3; 5 beats divided into 3 + 2; 8 beats divided into 5 + 3; 13 beats divided into 8 + 5. The music projects these segmentations by diverse means, above all harmonic rhythm. The expansions, in a texture of constant eighth notes so that their exact lengths become palpable, begin softly in a high register and progressively swoop down the cycle of fifths to ever louder climaxes in a low register before ascending again. Other streams with countervailing gestures emerge at preset temporal locations and attempt to escape this inexorable process, but they are engulfed by it.

After composing many pieces by expanding variations, it was natural to want to explore the reverse process, contracting variations. I first did this in several streams in *Quiet Music* that expand and then reverse. These streams are palindromes not of single events but of variation units. Figure 5.14 illustrates with a palindromic stream at the beginning of the work. Against it in faster note values is another stream (not shown) that expands without contraction and continues to develop after the palindrome closes off. The palindromic stream conveys stasis while the continuously expanding stream intensifies. This contrast in type of stream is itself part of the discourse.

The orchestra piece *Spirals* (2006) engages expanding-contracting variations in a more comprehensive form. In each of its two movements, as diagrammed in figure 5.15, the time spans and structural markers of the variations expand and spiral outward and then inward. However, as

aesthetic virtues or perceptual status of the golden section. I simply find the Fibonacci series occasionally useful for the nested self-similar groupings and asymmetrical rhythms that it affords.)

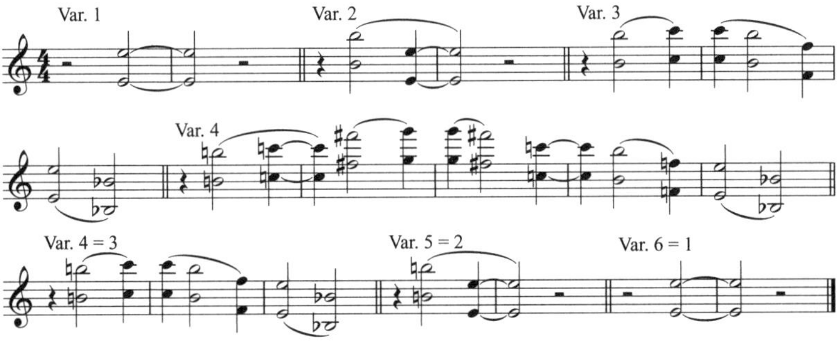

Figure 5.14. Palindromic expanding-contracting variations at the beginning of *Quiet Music.*

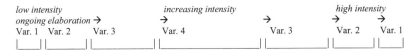

Figure 5.15. Palindromic expanding-contracting variations combined with continuous elaboration and intensification in *Spirals.*

the spiral reverses and contracts back to its point of origin, the musical ideas continue to elaborate. The combination of contracting spans and ongoing development culminates in moments of high intensity.

Expansion and contraction take the form of cantus firmus cycles in the chamber cello concerto *Arches* (2010) and the second movement, titled "Cycles," of the piano trio *Times 3* (2012). In both pieces, the internal structure of each cycle is palindromic, and so is the sequence of cycles. Figure 5.16a shows the first two cycles from *Times 3*. The Roman numerals above the staff mark the expanding-contracting canti firmi. The end of one cycle overlaps with the beginning of the next. The second cycle inserts a new expanded variation. The Arabic numerals beneath the staff mark the number of beats per variation, again by Fibonacci proportions.

Figure 5.16b displays with Fibonacci numbers the overall palindrome of the cycles. Against this diatonic scaffold, other musical strands weave

(a)

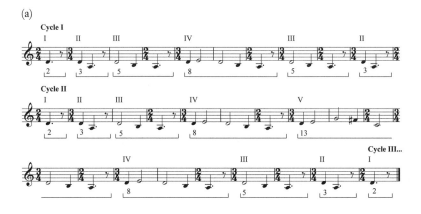

(b)

2 3 5 8 5 3 2 ‖ 2 3 5 8 13 8 5 3 2 ‖ 2 3 5 8 13 21 13 8 5 3 2 ‖ 2 3 5 8 13 8 5 3 2 ‖ 2 3 5 8 5 3 2
A   B   A'   B'   A''

Figure 5.16. Palindromic expanding-contracting cantus firmus in the second movement of *Times 3:* (a) the first two cycles, forming nested time spans in Fibonacci proportions; (b) the palindrome of cycles in Fibonacci-proportion time spans, creating an ABABA form.

a complex argument in ABABA form. In the A sections the cantus firmus is often in the foreground, but in the B sections it is partially disguised in the instrumental figuration.

One might ask why I wrote a diatonic cantus firmus. Beginning with *Fantasy Etudes,* the diatonic collection has attracted my intermittent compositional interest less for its historical or cultural associations than for its group-theoretic properties of uniqueness and maximal evenness and for the rich multidimensional pitch space that it is capable of projecting (see the discussions in chapters 2 and 3). In the case at hand, I wanted a cantus firmus that pointed toward its tonal center **G** without arriving on it. Resolution is thus withheld from variation to variation, propelling the music forward. The position-pointing potential of the diatonic collection, a consequence of its uniqueness property, fulfills this formal and expressive end.

(a)

(b)

(c)

Figure 5.17. Pitch-rhythm mappings in *The First Voices:* (a) progressive filling-out of the mapping in diatonic space, (b) modal rotation, (c) mappings in nondiatonic pitch spaces.

The diatonic collection is dealt with more fully in a piece that does not proceed in expanding (or contracting) variations, *The First Voices* (2007) for eight percussionists and three female singers. The text by Jean-Jacques Rousseau (1763) asserts the common origin of language and music in expressive prelinguistic vocalizations, similar to the argument in chapter 3, except that Rousseau's conception was pre-evolutionary. Much of the piece is based on the isomorphism between the diatonic scale and the common West African rhythm discussed in chapter 3. On this level, the piece is a meditation on the cognitive features behind the isomorphism. Figure 5.17a gives the mapping, following levels of the diatonic-triadic basic space and including a pentatonic level.[6] Each melodic interval measured in semitones translates into equivalent durational intervals. Figure 5.17b rotates the diatonic set

6. I originally wrote these rhythms in 12/8 meter, following African practice (see chapter 3), but renotated them in 3/2 to make them easier to perform for Western musicians. When composing the piece, I thought in terms not of 12/8 or 3/2 but of the durational patterns themselves.

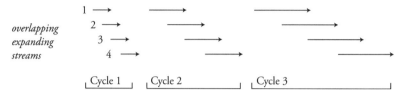

Figure 5.18. Expanding streams in *Time and Again,* both within each cycle and from one cycle to the next.

modally along with its rhythmic equivalents. Figure 5.17c translates the mapping into nondiatonic scales. An extended passage in *The First Voices* hypermodulates systematically through these alternative spaces.

Ever since I was a graduate student, I have regarded Babbitt's time-point system, which maps tone-row intervals onto equivalent spans under the usual serial operations, to be perceptually absurd. It therefore gave me satisfaction to compose what in effect is a time-point piece in which the pitch-rhythm mapping is perceivable.

In a further development of spiral form, the orchestra piece *Time and Again* (2014) builds expanding (and sometimes contracting) streams as before, but its global form comprises three sections that also expand, producing a double hierarchy of spirals. Figure 5.18 diagrams this process abstractly with four streams. Each arrow in cycle 1 stands for several expanding variations within its stream. Cycle 2 restarts the expansion from cycle 1 but in a more elaborated form, as represented by the longer arrows. The process continues in cycle 3.

In several passages, however, the process steps outside the framework of figure 5.18, creating at times a recitative-like conversational quality. These different treatments manipulate the temporal flow. *Time and Again* does this not only in customary ways, such as rate of events and harmonic rhythm, but also by the extent to which its musical ideas are palindromic, hence static; rigorously developmental, hence progressing forward step by step; or nonrigorously developmental, hence moving forward in somewhat unpredictable ways. The streams of contrasting ideas and textures often overlap, creating degrees of order and disorder that further shape the local sense of temporal flow. At a global level, the spiral-within-spiral form lends the flow a fatalistic coloring, as if the recurrences could continue indefinitely.

As a balance to its hybrid formal processes, the motivic materials in *Time and Again* are tightly related. They all come from the symmetrical voice leading of the quartet syntax and its S→D→T functions (see figure 5.1). Figures 5.19a–g illustrate with fragments taken from Cycle I. The work's opening flourish, sketched in figure 5.19a, twice iterates S→D before resolving D→T on the global tonic **A**. The passage in figure 5.19b extracts part of the whole-tone collection by the progression S→D, and 5.19c does likewise for a chromatic cluster by the progression D→T. The upper line of S→D→T appears in 5.19d and, transposed and repeated, forms an incomplete diatonic scale. The diatonic collection continues in 5.19e by a resetting of the symmetrical voice leading in 5.19a from unison to a major third apart. The passage in 5.19f slightly distorts the symmetry of the voice leading in 5.19a. In 5.19g, four-note segments of the whole-tone scale combine by ascending fifths to form a sequence of diatonic scales.

The melody in figure 5.19h appears at the end of Cycle III before a short coda. The brackets above the melody show its extent in Cycles I and II, respectively. It progressively expands at either end, so that by Cycle III it replicates the exact range (an octave lower) of the top line in 5.19a, with two subsidiary cadences followed by resolution on **A**. The piece begins and ends with the same material on different time scales.

This discussion of compositional procedures and their cognitive underpinnings has been selective, focusing on a formal level on expanding (and contracting) variations in mostly simple and pared-down contexts. In fact, about half the pieces in my oeuvre do not employ expanding variations. Whether they do or not depends on aesthetic and expressive goals. For me the crucial moment in composing a work is to find the form that fits the musical idea and make them one. If I have emphasized expanding variations, it is because it is my most characteristic formal procedure, one that I have made my own in a variety of ways, and because it is based on a fundamental cognitive principle, that

Figure 5.19. In the upper staff, fragments of musical ideas in *Time and Again;* in the lower staff, elements of motivic relatedness derived from the quartet syntax.

of hierarchical elaboration. It avoids imitation of traditional forms, yet (to use terminology from chapter 4) it yields complicated forms that are readily perceivable—that is, forms that are complex. Furthermore, it combines constraints and freedom in a satisfying way. A given variation establishes the framework for how the next variation can develop, but it does not prescribe the details of how it will develop. Once the next variation is composed, it sets the bounds for the variation after that. The past constrains the future but does not determine it.

It should be apparent that I do not use my work in music theory and cognition as a recipe for composition. Rather, the relationship between theory and composition is flexible, a source of ideas going in both directions. The theory serves above all as a framework for my musical and aesthetic thought. How I apply it varies from piece to piece. Some pieces, such as the string quartet cycle and *Time and Again,* are strictly conceived in some respects and somewhat unconstrained in others. Other pieces, such as the second movement of *Time after Time* and all of *Spirals,* are rigorously constructed throughout, yet in ways that sound completely natural. One of my ideals is to have a theory that is so in tune with the musical mind that its compositional application disappears in the music itself, leaving its trace everywhere and nowhere.

REFERENCES

Agawu, K. 2006. "Structural Analysis or Cultural Analysis? Competing Perspectives on the 'Standard Pattern' of West African Rhythm." *Journal of the American Musicological Society* 59, no. 1: 1–46.

Agmon, E. 1996. "Coherent Tone-Systems: A Study in the Theory of Diatonicism." *Journal of Music Theory* 40: 39–59.

Arnheim, R. 1954. *Art and Visual Perception*. Berkeley: University of California Press.

Arom, S. 1991. *African Polyphony and Polyrhythm: Musical Structure and Methodology*. Cambridge: Cambridge University Press.

Babbitt, M. 2003. *Collected Essays*. Edited by S. Peles. Princeton, NJ: Princeton University Press.

Baker, M.C. 2001. *The Atoms of Language*. New York: Basic Books.

Balzano, G.J. 1980. "The Group-Theoretic Description of 12-Fold and Microtonal Pitch Systems." *Computer Music Journal* 4, no. 4: 66–84.

———. 1982. "The Pitch Set as a Level of Description for Studying Musical Pitch Perception." In *Music, Mind, and Brain*, edited by M. Clynes. New York: Plenum.

Bernstein, L. 1976. *The Unanswered Question*. Cambridge, MA: Harvard University Press.

Bharucha, J.J. 1984a. "Anchoring Effects in Music: The Resolution of Dissonance." *Cognitive Psychology* 16: 485–518.

————. 1984b. "Event Hierarchies, Tonal Hierarchies, and Assimilation: A Reply to Deutsch and Dowling." *Journal of Experimental Psychology: General* 113: 421–25.

Bigand, E., R. Parncutt, and F. Lerdahl. 1996. "Perception of Musical Tension in Short Chord Sequences: The Influence of Harmonic Function, Sensory Dissonance, Horizontal Motion, and Musical Training." *Perception and Psychophysics* 58: 125–41.

Bigand, E., and M. Pineau. 1997. "Global Context Effects on Musical Expectancy." *Perception and Psychophysics* 59: 1098–107.

Boulez, P. 1971. *Boulez on Music Today.* Translated by S. Bradshaw. Cambridge, MA: Harvard University Press. Translation of P. Boulez, *Penser la musique aujourd'hui.* Paris: Mediations, 1964.

Boulez, P. 1991. *Stocktakings from an Apprenticeship.* Oxford: Clarendon. Translation of *Relevés d'apprenti.* Paris: Éditions du Seuil, 1966.

Bregman, A. S. 1990. *Auditory Scene Analysis.* Cambridge, MA: MIT Press.

Brown, S. 2000. "The 'Musilanguage' Model of Music Evolution." In *The Origins of Music,* edited by N. L. Wallin, B. Merker, and S. Brown. Cambridge, MA: MIT Press.

Browne, R. 1981. "Tonal Implications of the Diatonic Set." *In Theory Only* 5: 3–21.

Bürger, P. 1984. *Theory of the Avant-Garde.* Translated by M. Shaw. Minneapolis: University of Minnesota Press.

Burns, E. M., and W. D. Ward. 1984. "Intervals, Scales, and Tuning." In *The Psychology of Music,* edited by D. Deutsch, 241–70. New York: Academic.

Carey, S. 2009. *The Origin of Concepts.* New York: Oxford University Press.

Cariani, P. 2001. "Temporal Codes, Timing Nets, and Music Perception." *Journal of New Music Research* 30, no. 2: 107–35.

Carter, E. 2002. *Harmony Book.* New York: Carl Fischer.

Cetiz, M. 2017. "Evaluation of Hierarchical Pitch Organization in Turkish Makam." Unpublished manuscript.

Chomsky, N. 1965. *Aspects of the Theory of Syntax.* Cambridge, MA: MIT Press.

————. 1968. *Language and Mind.* Cambridge: Cambridge University Press. 3rd edition published in 2006.

Clarke, D. 2017. "North Indian Classical Music and Lerdahl and Jackendoff's Generative Theory—A Mutual Regard." *Music Theory Online* 23, no. 3: 1–30.

Clarke, E. 1999. "Rhythm and Timing in Music." In *The Psychology of Music,* 2nd ed., edited by D. Deutsch, 473–500. New York: Academic.

Clough, J., and J. Douthett. 1991. "Maximally Even Sets." *Journal of Music Theory* 35: 93–173.

Cohn, R. 2011. "Tonal Pitch Space and the (Neo)-Riemannian *Tonnetz*. In *The Oxford Handbook of Neo-Riemannian Music Theories,* edited by E. Gollin and A. Rehding. New York: Oxford University Press.

―――. 2012. *Audacious Euphony: Chromaticism and the Triad's Second Nature.* New York: Oxford University Press.

―――. 2013. Introduction to *David Lewin's Morgengruss: Text, Context, Commentary.* Edited by D. Bard-Schwarz and R. Cohn. New York: Oxford University Press.

Cone, E. T. 1968. *Musical Form and Musical Performance.* New York: Norton.

―――. 1982. "Schubert's Promissory Note: An Exercise in Musical Hermeneutics." *19th-Century Music 5,* no. 3: 233–41.

Cooper, G., and L. B. Meyer. 1960. *The Rhythmic Structure of Music.* Chicago: University of Chicago Press.

Damasio, A. 1999. *The Feeling of What Happens: Body and Emotion in the Making of Consciousness.* New York: Harcourt Brace.

Darwin, C. 1871. *The Descent of Man and Selection in Relation to Sex.* London: John Murray.

Dehaene, S. 1997. *The Number Sense.* Oxford: Oxford University Press.

Deliège, I. 1987. "Grouping Conditions in Listening to Music: An Approach to Lerdahl and Jackendoff's Grouping Preference Rules." *Music Perception* 4: 325–60.

Dibben, N. 1994. "The Cognitive Reality of Hierarchic Structure in Tonal and Atonal Music." *Music Perception* 12: 1–25.

Doelling, K. B., and D. Poeppel. 2015. "Cortical Entrainment to Music and Its Modulation by Expertise." *Proceedings of the National Academy of Science,* published online October 26, 2015. www.pnas.org/content/112/45/E6233.

Euler, L. 1739. *Tentamen novae theoriae musicae.* Saint Petersburg; New York: Broude, 1968.

Fitch, W. T. 2006. "The Biology and Evolution of Music: A Comparative Perspective." *Cognition* 100: 173–215.

―――. 2010. *The Evolution of Language.* Cambridge: Cambridge University Press.

Forte, A. 1973. *The Structure of Atonal Music.* New Haven, CT: Yale University Press.

Frankland, B. W., and A. J. Cohen. 2004. "Parsing of Melody: Quantification and Testing of the Local Grouping Rules of Lerdahl and Jackendoff's *A Generative Theory of Tonal Music. Music Perception* 21: 499–543.

Gamer, C. 1967. "Some Combinatorial Resources of Equal-Tempered Systems." *Journal of Music Theory* 11, no. 1: 32–59.

Gibson, J. J. 1966. *The Senses Considered as Perceptual Systems*. New York: Houghton Mifflin.

Gilmore, B. 1995. "Changing the Metaphor: Ratio Models of Musical Pitch in the Work of Harry Partch, Ben Johnston, and James Tenney." *Perspectives of New Music* 33: 458–503.

Gjerdingen, R. 2007. *Music in the Galant Style*. New York: Oxford University Press.

Gollin, E., and A. Rehding, eds. 2011. *The Oxford Handbook of Neo-Riemannian Music Theories*. New York: Oxford University Press.

Hamanaka, M., K. Hirata, and S. Tojo. 2006. "Implementing 'A Generative Theory of Tonal Music.'" *Journal of New Music Research* 35, no. 4: 249–77.

Hasegawa, R. 2009. "Gérard Grisey and the 'Nature' of Harmony." *Music Analysis* 28, no. 2–3: 349–71.

Hauser, M., and E. Spelke. 2004. "Evolutionary and Developmental Foundations of Human Knowledge: A Case Study of Mathematics." In *The Cognitive Neurosciences*, 3rd ed., edited by M. Gazzaniga. Cambridge, MA: MIT Press.

Heider, F., and M. Simmel. 1944. "An Experimental Study of Apparent Behavior." *American Journal of Psychology* 57: 243–59.

Heinemann, S. 1998. "Pitch-Class Set Multiplication in Theory and Practice." *Music Theory Spectrum* 20, no. 1: 72–96.

Hervé, J.-L. 2009. "Quatre chants pour franchir le seuil." In *Contemporary Compositional Techniques and OpenMusic*. Paris: Delatour.

Hindemith, P. (1937) 1942. *The Craft of Musical Composition*. Vol. 1. New York: Belwin-Mills.

Hirata, K., and T. Aoyagi. 2003. "Computational Music Representation Based on the Generative Theory of Tonal Music and the Deductive Object-Oriented Database." *Computer Music Journal* 27, no. 3: 73–89.

Honing, H., ed. 2018. *The Origins of Musicality*. Cambridge, MA: MIT Press.

Huron, D. 2001. "Tone and Voice: A Derivation of the Rules of Voice-Leading from Perceptual Principles." *Music Perception*, 19, no. 1: 1–64.

———. 2006. *Sweet Expectation: Music and the Psychology of Expectation*. Cambridge, MA: MIT Press.

Husserl, E. 1964. *The Phenomenology of Internal Time-Consciousness*. Translated by J. S. Churchill. Edited by M. Heidegger. Bloomington: Indiana University Press.

Hutchinson, W., and L. Knopoff. 1978. "The Acoustical Component of Western Consonance." *Interface* 7: 1–29.

Jackendoff, R. 1977. *X-Syntax: A Study of Phrase Structure.* Cambridge, MA: MIT Press.

———. 1983. *Semantics and Cognition.* Cambridge, MA: MIT Press.

———. 1991. "Musical Parsing and Musical Affect." *Music Perception* 9: 199–230.

———. 2002. *Foundations of Language.* New York: Oxford University Press.

———. 2009. "Parallels and Nonparallels between Language and Music." *Music Perception* 26: 195–204.

Jackendoff, R., and F. Lerdahl. 2006. "The Capacity for Music: What Is It, and What's Special About It?" *Cognition* 100: 33–72.

Kassler, M. 1963. "A Sketch of the Use of Formalized Languages for the Assertion of Music." *Perspectives of New Music* 1, no. 2: 83–94.

Katz, J., and D. Pesetsky. 2011. "The Identity Thesis for Language and Music." https://ling.auf.net/lingbuzz/000959.

Koblyakov, L. 1977. "P. Boulez, 'Le marteau sans maître': Analysis of Pitch Structure." *Zeitschrift für Musiktheorie* 8, no. 1: 24–39.

———. 1993. *Pierre Boulez: A World of Harmony.* New York: Routledge.

Koelsch, S., M. Rohrmeier, R. Torrescuso, and S. Jentschke. 2013. "Processing of Hierarchical Syntactic Structure in Music." *Proceedings of the National Academy of Sciences* 110, no. 38: 15443–48.

Koffka, K. 1935. *Principles of Gestalt Psychology.* New York: Harcourt, Brace, and World.

Komar, A. 1971. *Theory of Suspensions.* Princeton, NJ: Princeton University Press.

Krumhansl, C. L. 1983. "Perceptual Structures for Tonal Music." *Music Perception* 1: 28–62.

———. 1990. *Cognitive Foundations of Musical Pitch.* New York: Oxford University Press.

———. 1996. "A Perceptual Analysis of Mozart's Piano Sonata K. 282: Segmentation, Tension, and Musical Ideas." *Music Perception* 13: 401–32.

Krumhansl, C. L., and E. Kessler. 1982. "Tracing the Dynamic Changes in Perceived Tonal Organization in a Spatial Representation of Musical Keys." *Psychological Review* 89: 334–68.

Kubik, G. 2010. *Theory of African Music.* Vol. 2. Chicago: University of Chicago Press.

Large, E. W., and C. Palmer. 2002. "Perceiving Temporal Regularity in Music." *Cognitive Science* 26: 1–37.

Large, E., and J. S. Snyder. 2009. "Pulse and Meter as Neural Resonance." *Neurosciences and Music III—Disorders and Plasticity: Annals of the New York Academy of Sciences* 1169: 46–57.

Larson, S. 2004. "Musical Forces and Melodic Expectations: Comparing Computer Models and Experimental Results." *Music Perception* 21: 457–98.

———. 2012. *Musical Forces: Motion, Metaphor, and Meaning in Music*. Bloomington: Indiana University Press.

Lerdahl, F. 1987. "Timbral Hierarchies." *Contemporary Music Review* 1: 135–60.

———. 1988a. "Cognitive Constraints on Compositional Systems." In *Generative Processes in Music*, edited by J. Sloboda. Oxford: Oxford University Press. Reprinted in *Contemporary Music Review* 6 (1991): 97–121. French edition: *Contrechamps* 10 (1988): 25–57.

———. 1988b. "Tonal Pitch Space." *Music Perception* 5: 315–50.

———. 1996. "Tonality and Paranoia: A Reply to Boros." *Perspectives of New Music* 34, no. 1: 242–51.

———. 1999. "Composing Notes." *Current Musicology* 67/68: 243–51.

——— 2001a. "The Sounds of Poetry Viewed as Music." *Annals of the New York Academy of Sciences* 930: 337–54. Reprinted in R.J. Zatorre and I. Peretz, eds. *The Biological Foundations of Music*. New York: Oxford University Press, 2001.

———. 2001b. *Tonal Pitch Space*. New York: Oxford University Press.

———. 2008. "On Carter's Influence." In *Elliott Carter: A Centennial Celebration*, edited by M. Ponthus and S. Tang, 15–22. Hillsdale, NY: Pendragon Press.

———. 2009. "Genesis and Architecture of the GTTM Project." *Music Perception* 26: 187–94.

———. 2013. "Musical Syntax and Its Relation to Linguistic Syntax." In *Language, Music, and the Brain: A Mysterious Relationship*, edited by M.A. Arbib. Strüngmann Forum Reports, vol. 10, 257–72. J. Lupp, series ed. Cambridge, MA: MIT Press.

———. 2015a. "Concepts and Representations of Musical Hierarchies." *Music Perception* 33: 83–95.

———. 2015b. "Structure and Ambiguity in a Schumann Song." In *Structures in the Mind: Essays on Language, Music, and Cognition in Honor of Ray Jackendoff*, edited by I. Toivonen, P. Csúri, and E. van der Zee, 347–69. Cambridge, MA: MIT Press.

Lerdahl, F., and R. Jackendoff. 1983. *A Generative Theory of Tonal Music*. Cambridge, MA: MIT Press.

Lerdahl, F., and C.L. Krumhansl. 2007. "Modeling Tonal Tension." *Music Perception* 24, no. 4: 329–66.

Lewin, D. (1974) 2013. *Morgengruss*. In David Lewin's *Morgengruss: Text, Context, Commentary*, edited by D. Bard-Schwarz and R. Cohn. New York: Oxford University Press.

London, J. 2012. *Hearing in Time: Psychological Aspects of Musical Meter.* New York: Oxford University Press.

Macklay, S. 2014. "Poetic, Harmonic, and Rhythmic Organization in *Quatre chants,* I." Unpublished manuscript.

Mann, T. 1961. *The Story of a Novel: The Genesis of Doctor Faustus.* Translated by R. Winston and C. Winston. New York: Alfred A. Knopf.

Marsden, A. 2005. "Generative Structural Representations of Tonal Music." *Journal of New Music Research* 34, no. 4: 409–28.

McAdams, S. 1989. "Psychological Constraints on Form-Bearing Dimensions in Music." *Contemporary Music Review* 4: 181–98.

McCarthy, J.J. 2001. *A Thematic Guide to Optimality Theory.* Cambridge: Cambridge University Press.

Messiaen, O. 1944. *Technique de mon langage musical.* Paris: Alphonse Leduc.

Meyer, L. B. 1956. *Emotion and Meaning in Music.* Chicago: University of Chicago Press.

———. 1967. *Music, the Arts, and Ideas.* Chicago: University of Chicago Press. 2nd edition published in 1994.

———. 1973. *Explaining Music.* Berkeley: University of California Press.

Murail, T. 2005. "Models and Artifice: The Collected Writings of Tristan Murail." *Contemporary Music Review* 24, no. 2/3.

Narmour, E. 1990. *The Analysis and Cognition of Basic Melodic Structures.* Chicago: University of Chicago Press.

Neisser, U. 1967. *Cognitive Psychology.* Englewood Cliffs, NJ: Prentice-Hall.

Oettingen, A. von. 1866. *Harmoniesystem in dualer Entwickelung.* Dorpat: Glaser.

Palmer, C., and C.L. Krumhansl. 1987. "Independent Temporal and Pitch Structures in Determination of Musical Phrases." *Journal of Experimental Psychology: Human Perception and Performance* 13: 116–26.

———. 1990. "Mental Representations for Musical Meter." *Journal of Experimental Psychology: Human Perception and Performance* 16: 728–41.

Parncutt, R. 1989. *Harmony: A Psychoacoustical Approach.* Berlin: Springer-Verlag.

Patel, A.D. 2003. "Language, Music, Syntax, and the Brain." *Nature Neuroscience* 6, no. 7: 674–81.

———. 2008. *Music, Language, and the Brain.* New York: Oxford University Press.

———. 2009. "Musical Rhythm, Linguistic Rhythm, and Human Evolution." *Music Perception* 24, no. 1: 99–104.

———. 2010. "Music, Biological Evolution, and the Brain." In *Emerging Disciplines,* edited by M. Bailar. Houston, TX: Rice University Press.

Patel, A.D., J.R. Iverson, M.R. Bregman, and I. Schulz. 2009. "Experimental Evidence for Synchronization to a Musical Beat in a Nonhuman Animal." *Current Biology* 19: 827–30.

Peel, J., and W. Slawson. 1984. "Review of A Generative Theory of Tonal Music." *Journal of Music Theory* 28: 271–94.

Peretz, I., and M. Coltheart. 2003. "Modularity of Music Processing." *Nature Neuroscience* 6: 688–91.

Perle, G. 1991. *The Listening Composer.* Berkeley: University of California Press.

Pinker, S. 1997. *How the Mind Works.* New York: Norton.

Pressing, J. 1983. "Cognitive Isomorphisms between Pitch and Rhythm in World Musics: West Africa, the Balkans, and Western Tonality." *Studies in Music* 17: 38–61.

Pressnitzer, D., S. McAdams, S. Winsberg, and J. Fineberg. 2000. "Perception of Musical Tension for Nontonal Orchestral Timbres and Its Relation to Psychoacoustic Roughness." *Perception and Psychophysics* 62: 66–80.

Rahn, J. 1983. *A Theory for All Music: Problems and Solutions in the Analysis of Non-Western Forms.* Toronto: University of Toronto Press.

Reich, S. 2004. *Writings on Music.* Edited by P. Hillier. New York: Oxford University Press.

Riemann, H. 1882. "Die Natur der Harmonik." *Sammlung musikalische Vorträge* 4, no. 40. Leipzig: Breitkopf und Härtel, 157–90.

———. 1893. *Vereinfachte Harmonielehre; oder, Die Lehre von den tonalen Funktionen der Akkorde.* London: Augener.

———. 1915. "Ideen zu einer 'Lehre von der Tonvorstellungen.'" *Musikbibliothek Peters* 21–22: 1–26.

Rings, S. 2011. *Tonality and Transformation.* New York: Oxford University Press.

Rodet, X., Y. Potard, and J.-B. Barrière. 1984. "The CHANT Project: From Synthesis of the Singing Voice to Synthesis in General." *Computer Music Journal* 8, no. 3: 15–31.

Rohrmeier, M. 2011. "Towards a Generative Syntax of Tonal Harmony." *Journal of Mathematics and Music* 5, no. 1: 35–53.

Rosch, E. 1975. "Cognitive Reference Points." *Cognitive Psychology* 7: 532–47.

Rosch, E., and C.B. Mervis. 1975. "Family Resemblances: Studies in the Internal Structure of Categories." *Cognitive Psychology* 7: 573–605.

Rothstein, W. 1989. *Phrase Rhythm in Tonal Music.* New York: Schirmer.

Rousseau, J.J. 1763. *Essai sur l'origine des langues.* In *Oeuvres completes de J.J. Rousseau,* tome troisième. Paris: Furne, 1852.

Sabat, M. 2016. "Three Tables for Bob." *Tempo* 70, no. 278: 47–63.

Salzer, F. 1952. *Structural Hearing: Tonal Coherence in Music*. New York: Charles Boni. Reprint, New York: Dover, 1962.

Schachter, C. 1980. "Rhythm and Linear Analysis: Durational Reduction." In *The Music Forum*, vol. 4, edited by F. Salzer. New York: Columbia University Press.

Schaeffer, P. 1966. *Traité des objets musicaux*. Paris: Éditions du Seuil. Translated by C. North and J. Dack as *Treatise on Musical Objects*. California Studies in 20th-Century Music. Berkeley: University of California Press, 2017.

Schenker, H. 1921–24. *Der Tonwille*. Vienna: A. Gutmann Verlag.

———. 1935. *Der freie Satz: Neue Musikalische Theorien under Phantasien*. Vol. 3. Vienna: Universal Edition. Translated by E. Oster as *Free Composition*. New York: Longman, 1979.

Schlenker, P. 2017. "Outline of Musical Semantics." *Music Perception* 35: 3–37.

Schoenberg, A. (1911) 1978. *Theory of Harmony*. Translated by R. Carter. Berkeley: University of California Press.

———. (1950) 1975. *Style and Idea*. New York: St. Martin's Press.

———. (1954) 1969. *Structural Functions of Harmony*. Rev. ed. New York: Norton.

———. (1965) 1987. *Letters*. Edited by E. Stein. Berkeley: University of California Press.

Smalley, D. 1997. "Spectromorphology: Explaining Sound-Shapes." *Organised Sound* 2, no. 2: 107–26.

Smith, N. A., and L. L. Cuddy. 2003. "Perceptions of Musical Dimensions in Beethoven's *Waldstein* Sonata: An Application of Tonal Pitch Space Theory." *Musicae Scientiae* 7: 7–34.

Stevens, S. S. 1946. "Measurement Scales and Statistics: A Clash of Paradigms." *Psychological Bulletin* 100, no. 3: 398–407.

Stravinsky, I., and R. Craft. 1959. *Expositions and Developments*. Berkeley: University of California Press.

Stuckenschmidt, H. H. 1978. *Schoenberg: His Life, World, and Work*. New York: Macmillan.

Temperley, D. 2001. *The Cognition of Basic Musical Structures*. Cambridge, MA: MIT Press.

———. 2007. *Music and Probability*. Cambridge, MA: MIT Press.

———. 2014. "Information Flow and Repetition in Music." *Journal of Music Theory* 58: 155–78.

Terhardt, E. 1974. "Pitch, Consonance, and Harmony." *Journal of the Acoustical Society of America* 55: 1061–69.

————. 1984. "The Concept of Musical Consonance: A Link between Music and Psychoacoustics." *Music Perception* 1, no. 3: 276–95.

Terhardt, E., G. Stoll, and M. Seewann. 1982. "Pitch of Complex Tonal Signals According to Virtual Pitch Theory: Tests, Examples, and Predictions." *Journal of the Acoustical Society of America* 71: 671–78.

Thoresen, L. 2007. "Spectromorphological Analysis of Sound Objects: An Adaptation of Pierre Schaeffer's Typomorphology." *Organised Sound* 12, no. 2: 129–41.

Travis, R. 1966. "Directed Motion in Schoenberg and Webern." *Perspectives of New Music* 4: 85–89.

Tymoczko, D. 2011. *A Geometry of Music: Harmony and Counterpoint in the Extended Common Practice.* New York: Oxford University Press.

Wallin, N.L., B. Merker, and S. Brown, eds. 2001. *The Origins of Music.* Cambridge, MA: MIT Press.

Weber, G. 1821–24. *Versuch einer geordeneten Theorie der Tonsetzkunst.* Mainz: B. Schotts Söhne.

Westergaard, P. 1975. *An Introduction to Tonal Theory.* New York: Norton.

Wittgenstein, L. 1953. *Philosophical Investigations.* Oxford: Blackwell.

Yust, J. 2015. "Voice-Leading Transformation and Generative Theories of Tonal Structure." *Music Theory Online* 21, no. 4: 1–21.

————. 2018. *Organized Time: Rhythm, Tonality, and Form.* New York: Oxford University Press.

Zuckerkandl, V. 1956. *Sound and Symbol.* Translated by W.R. Trask. Princeton, NJ: Princeton University Press.

INDEX

Adorno, T. W., 9
Aesthetic claims, 82–83
African rhythm, 7, 60–63, 69, 125
Agency, 69–71
Associative structure, 24, 52, 90, 95
Attractions: tonal, 12–13, 15, 44–46, 46n,
   48n, 51, 69–70, 72, 74, 98, 107, 109,
   116–118, 121; metrical, 69
Auditory scenes, 54
Avant-garde, 5, 83, 83n

Babbitt, M., 2–3, 9–10, 77, 86, 103–104,
   126
Bach, J. S., 44, 55, 88
Balzano, G., 64
Bartók, B., 9, 11, 18, 65
Beethoven, L. van: 77; Fifth Symphony,
   57, 88; Ninth Symphony, 43; piano
   sonatas, 55
Berio, L., 1
Berlioz, H., 97
Bernstein, L., 5–6; *The Unanswered
   Question*, 5
Bharucha, J. J., 39, 45
Boulez, P., 1, 3, 78, 86, 105–106, 112, 117; *Le
   marteau sans maître*, 78, 84, 88
Bregman, A. S., 54–55

Cage, J., 5
Cariani, P., 72
Carter, E., 1, 3, 6, 117; Second String
   Quartet, 89–90
Chomsky, N., 20–21, 31, 53; *Language and
   Mind*, 4
Clarke, D., 72
Cognitive opacity, 78n, 81–82
Cognitive reference points, 71–74,
   84–85
Cohn, R., 32n, 42n
Complexity and complicatedness, 83,
   87–88, 90
Cone, E. T., 49
Consonance and dissonance, 8, 14, 41,
   64, 67–68, 74, 81–82, 85, 107–108,
   112–113, 120
Constraints: cognitive, 78–83;
   preferential constraints on basic
   spaces, 67–69

Damasio, A., 70
Darwin, C.: 76; Darwinian adaptation,
   72
Debussy, C., 9, 11, 18, 65; "Voiles," 65
Deliège: C., 85
Del Tredici, D., 9

141

Founded in 1893,
UNIVERSITY OF CALIFORNIA PRESS
publishes bold, progressive books and journals
on topics in the arts, humanities, social sciences,
and natural sciences—with a focus on social
justice issues—that inspire thought and action
among readers worldwide.

The UC PRESS FOUNDATION
raises funds to uphold the press's vital role
as an independent, nonprofit publisher, and
receives philanthropic support from a wide
range of individuals and institutions—and from
committed readers like you. To learn more, visit
ucpress.edu/supportus.